Living
LARGE
on Less

A Guide to Saving
Without Sacrifice

Christina Spence

B

BETTERWAY HOME
CINCINNATI, OHIO
WWW.BETTERWAYBOOKS.COM

Living Large on Less: A Guide to Saving Without Sacrifice. Copyright © 2010 by Christina Spence. Manufactured in China. All rights reserved. No part of this book may be reproduced in any form or by any electronic or mechanical means including information storage and retrieval systems without permission in writing from the publisher, except by a reviewer who may quote brief passages in a review. The content of this book has been thoroughly reviewed for accuracy. However, the author and publisher disclaim any liability for any damages, losses or injuries that may result from the use or misuse of any product or information presented herein. It is the purchaser's responsibility to read and follow all instructions and warnings on all product labels. Published by Betterway Home Books, an imprint of F+W Media, Inc., 4700 East Galbraith Road, Cincinnati, Ohio, 45236. (800) 289-0963. First Edition.

Other fine Betterway Home Books are available from your local bookstore, or online, or direct from the publisher. Visit our Web site, www.fwmedia.com.

14   13   12   11   10   5   4   3   2   1

Distributed in Canada by Fraser Direct
100 Armstrong Avenue, Georgetown, Ontario, Canada L7G 5S4, Tel: (905) 877-4411

Distributed in the U.K. and Europe by F+W Media International
Brunel House, Newton Abbot, Devon, TQ12 4PU, England, Tel: (+44) 1626 323200,
Fax: (+44) 1626 323319, E-mail: postmaster@davidandcharles.co.uk

Distributed in Australia by Capricorn Link
P.O. Box 704, S. Windsor NSW, 2756 Australia, Tel: (02) 4577-3555

Library of Congress Cataloging in Publication Data
Spence, Christina,
   Living large on less : a guide to saving without sacrifice / by Christina Spence. -- 1st ed.
      p. cm.
   Includes index.
   ISBN 978-1-4403-0432-3 (pbk. : alk. paper)
   1. Thriftiness. 2. Finance, Personal. 3. Consumer education. I. Title.
   HG179.S55293 2010
   332.024--dc22
                                  2009053580

Edited by Jacqueline Musser; Designed by Clare Finney; Production coordinated by Mark Griffin

About the Author

Christina lives in Calgary, Alberta,
Canada with her husband and two
cats. They're all proud to be frugal,
even the cats. This is Christina's second
book with Betterway Home Books. Her
first, *No-Hassle Housecleaning*, was
published in 2009. Visit her Web site at
www.happyslob.com.

ACKNOWLEDGMENTS

A huge "Thank You!" to my editor, Jacqueline Musser. You are incredible at what you do, and you make my books come alive. More thanks go out to F+W for publishing this, my second book with them.

DEDICATION

TO COLIN, the coolest and kindest human I've ever known. (Thanks boo, for your endless patience with me. Especially during this project!) To my family and friends, who provide supportive words and limitless hugs.

Contents

Introduction

Does it feel like you've lost control of your finances? Do bills pile up unpaid? Have you been receiving those disturbing telephone calls from collectors that leave you unable to answer the phone? Or, maybe the situation isn't that dire, yet you still feel like money pours out of your hands like the proverbial sands through the hourglass. If it feels like your money is in control of you and not the other way around, then you'll find that making some of the changes outlined in *Living Large on Less* will come as a huge relief. You'll take a good hard look at your true financial situation, and you'll start taking steps to spend money more wisely and, therefore, make the money stretch to meet your needs.

Every major personal expense category is covered here, from housing and utilities to clothing and accessories to eating in and out, and even hobbies and vacations. In every area, you'll learn valuable tips on how to reduce how much you spend so that there will be more left over for debt repayment or savings and investments.

The concept of living large means different things to different people. Some might envision a huge home with a swimming pool in the backyard. Some might imagine a dream retirement where there's enough money to cover the basics and provide some little luxuries. I define the phrase "living large" as a good, balanced life with less financial worries. A large life is both fulfilling and tempered with financial responsibility. It finds a happy balance between fiscal awareness and reasonableness. And there's a healthy dose of fun in this kind of life, too!

So, come along with me on this interesting look into a life lived large—a life that you'll love, and one that you can actually afford! You'll learn how to balance the necessities, activities and hobbies you love with financial accountability. Far from being a restrictive life, it's one that will free you from the slavery of debt and money worries.

1 | Why Choose To Save?

Frugality is so *right now*. It's a topic discussed with flair and enthusiasm among people who not so long ago reserved such reverent tones for only brand names.

But what is frugality? A simple definition of frugality is the ability to stretch your money by not being wasteful with resources and by not spending unnecessarily. Beyond being a trend, frugality is an incredible lifestyle choice that will never go out of style. If you've picked up this book, then you're obviously looking for ways to save money without sacrificing a lot of your lifestyle. You want to be financially responsible, but not live like a pauper. Money-wise living will help you achieve that goal.

Perhaps the reason you've never delved into saving money before is because you thought *I'm just not the type to be frugal!* What do you envision when you think of a frugal person, anyway? Shocking! I assure you that we're not all clothed in fashions ten (or twenty) years out of date and with hair down to our belly buttons. We're also not penny-pinching misers, scowling every time we spend a nickel and certainly not willing to dole out for a good cause. In fact, someone frugal looks very much like, well, you. Look in a mirror, and voilà, you see the face of frugal living today. So, rid yourself of any preconceived perception of what frugality really entails, and you may very well surprise yourself with how much you love the freedom of living within your means.

> **Look in a mirror, and voilà, you see the face of frugal living today.**

REASONS TO START SAVING NOW

To get you started on your money-saving adventures, here is a list of reasons to spend less (while still living it up, of course). Check each point that applies to you. You might discover more reasons for saving money than you'd originally thought.

- ☐ To be able to make a large, important purchase, like a home.

- ☐ To retire at the age you choose while still maintaining the lifestyle you enjoy.

- ☐ To get out of debt.

- ☐ To reduce stress. We all know debt can lead to anxiety. A healthy bank account gives you tremendous peace of mind. Plus trying to keep up with the Joneses (who may in fact only be "successful" on the surface) is incredibly stressful. Learning to be content makes a person a lot happier in the end.

- ☐ To provide an education fund for your children.

- [ ] To stay home to raise your children. Relying on one income means frugality is suddenly a necessity.

- [ ] To be less wasteful.

- [ ] To appreciate what you already have. You don't want to weigh your life down with more stuff. (I call it UG—useless garbage.) It's more clutter to deal with later on. Whether it's a new plasma TV or another small appliance in the kitchen, it's all just accumulated stuff. The more stuff you have, the more time it takes to care for, maintain and fix that stuff when it breaks. So, a simpler life means a life less cluttered, and one you can be more efficient in.

- [ ] To get out of the "drone-like" consumerism of this world: Go to work, struggle at a job you hate, commute home, eat, watch a little TV and go to bed. Fewer expenses leave you freer to accomplish other goals and, perhaps, can free you from a job that you can't stand.

- [ ] To live a healthier lifestyle. How? You'll dine out less and enjoy simpler activities like good old walking.

- [ ] To give of both your time and your resources. If you're careful with money, you'll have a little extra to help someone else.

- [ ] To be more environmentally aware, because less consumption is easier on the planet.

- [ ] To learn resourcefulness. Look at how past generations dealt with money difficulties. They didn't sit around and complain about it, they got creative with it!

☐ To challenge yourself. (Getting all you can for your money is a fun challenge to undertake.)

THE NEW FINANCIAL REALITY

Why choose to start saving now? Why not continue to enjoy yourself and worry about the consequences later? Why has saving and living within one's means suddenly become a viable option?

We have accumulated more debt than our grandparents could've ever conceived.

The answer likely lies in our new awareness—we're now all well aware that our financial world has changed, maybe forever. Only a few years ago, many of us felt the freedom to charge pricey gadgets, clothes and furniture on our credit cards with nary a backward glance or thought. New, lavish homes with more bedrooms and bathrooms than we'd ever dreamt of were within our reach, even though they weren't really within our budget. We snatched up gorgeous, sleek new cars, even if the monthly cost of such vehicles went beyond our ability to pay. We thought we would worry about all that later.

Later is now. For many of us, changing the way we spend has become a necessity, no longer something we can put off. In North America, we have accumulated more debt than our grandparents could've ever conceived. We hardly blinked an eye when taking on mortgages of upwards of a half million dollars or more. And student loans, well, we figured that those were logical investments in our future success, so how could we possibly go wrong? If we hadn't figured out in advance the educational path that would work for us and help us secure employment, we could go very, very wrong indeed.

Debt seems like an unavoidable reality for Generation X (people

My History of Living Large on Less

So, why am I writing this book, and why should you listen to me? I guess I could say that I'm a naturally born frugalite, that is, a person who likes to get good value for every dollar spent. My parents are incredible examples of frugal living, and they always instilled in me the value of a dollar. Growing up, I watched them as they lived good, frugal lives, and I admired them. But in my early twenties, I thought that good old Mom and Dad were so old-fashioned that it was painful. I thought I knew how to handle my money better than they did.

Along with my ridiculous "insights" came a student loan. And credit card debt. Like so many others, I'd passed by the reasonable ideas of my parents and decided that debt was just a foregone conclusion. To get ahead you had to take on debt first, right? Right?

Wrong-o, my friend! Learning this lesson the hard way hurt at the time, but it's done me a world of good. Now, I carefully keep track of every single cent I spend. (Yes, even if people think I'm a little odd

born between 1965 and 1981) and Generation Y (people born in the early 1980s through the late 1990s), something that past generations never considered normal. Irresponsible spending isn't the only place to lay blame. Housing, education and health care costs have sky-rocketed in the last thirty years, leaving many with no option but to borrow if they want to attend school or buy a home. But, while costs are soaring, the typical full-time salary hasn't headed sky high, but has headed in the opposite direction. In inflation-adjusted dollars, full-time salaries have actually decreased over the past thirty years.

for doing it. I'll show you later how to turn those naysayers into fellow money-saving devotees.) I have a budget that I stick to. My husband and I work as a team to keep our finances healthier, and we're still working to pay off lingering debt. But, instead of being victims, we're in the battle together and are willing to work as hard as necessary to get rid of our debt forever, and never get caught in that trap again.

So, in short, my parents were right all along! (I can just imagine my dad's smug smirk as he reads that sentence, but I admit that it's true.) Save to pay for big purchases; don't needlessly plunk that charge on a credit card. You can live well within your means and have a great time doing it. You won't miss a thing, except all that nasty, nightmare-riddled debt that may very well be the reason why you picked up this book in the first place. So, come along with me and see firsthand how you can live large on less.

Debt and financial issues certainly weigh heavy on Gen X and Y:

- A study by Charles Schwab in 2008 found that 45 percent of Gen X state that they have too much debt to even think about saving.
- A 2008 Internet survey conducted by AARP and the American Savings Education Council found that 67 percent of Gen Xers had credit card debt, 52 percent had car loans, 49 percent had mortgages, 30 percent had student loans, 28 percent had medical debt and 16 percent had home equity loans.

15

1
WHY CHOOSE TO SAVE?

- In a study conducted by Fidelity Investments in 2008, when asked what keeps them up at night, 77 percent of Gen X and 74 percent of Gen Y named money as their biggest concern, well above concern over family or health care.
- The same Fidelity study found that Gens X and Y agree that saving for retirement is a goal, but other financial priorities and managing debt is more crucial.

> **45 percent of Gen Xers state that they have too much debt to even think about saving.**

START SAVING TODAY

This book is not about dwelling on all of the mistakes we've made. If you are in debt, you certainly have to acknowledge that you've made some errors, face the reality of the financial situation you're going to dig yourself out from under, and then get on with it. Chapter three will help you formulate a specific plan to do just that. *Living Large on Less* will help you spend less and save more, and you can use that savings for a number of important things. In addition to paying off debt, maybe you want to stay at home to raise your children or reduce your financial worries. Or maybe you are recovering from bankruptcy, lost your job or had your income or investment values reduced. A lifestyle of money wisdom is a perfect option for you no matter what your financial situation is.

Even if you've tightened your financial belt before, you'll find many new and unique money-saving suggestions and ideas in this book. If you're trying a more frugal lifestyle for the very first time, good for you! You'll find that it's a journey that is surprisingly fun. Frugal living isn't about cutting out all the nice things from your

The Beauty of Reasonableness

If you're struggling with debt or want to learn to save rather than spend every cent that comes your way, you're in luck. Living large on less means you'll live a happier life, and one that's more balanced. Spending every cent you make isn't balanced. On the other hand, for most of us, living on canned beans and rice isn't balanced. Frugality and fun can meet in the middle. Financially speaking, it's what I like to call the beauty of reasonableness.

life, it's about learning what you truly need to live (the necessities), and then adding a few nice extras here and there. The nice extras aren't the main core of your spending, just as chocolate isn't the main core of our diets. (I know, I know, we'd all like it to be, but we just know better.)

SPENDING CHALLENGE

A variety of spending challenges are sprinkled throughout the book. Undertaking these challenges will not only make your savings account sigh with happiness, but will also teach you some valuable new skills along the way—namely budget consciousness. Budget consciousness doesn't mean that you'll never spend money again, but you'll become much more aware of how that spending affects your bottom line. And, on top of all that, the spending challenges make your new money management routine fun.

You can be romantic, spontaneous, fashionable, creative and quirky all while spending less money. Frugality frees you to get out and enjoy life more, instead of relying on spending and consumption as your only types of entertainment. You can enjoy picnics, play pick-up games of football in the backyard with friends, watch old movies, or renew your interest in a long-neglected hobby without spending a dime. You can make more delicious meals at home instead of always relying on takeout. You'll be more inspired than ever, and soon won't even remember why shopping and consuming seemed so important before.

Living Large on Less offers a very balanced approach to saving and being frugal. This is not an insanely restrictive approach to saving money, where you can never go out to eat at a restaurant or out to a movie with your pals. It's about enjoying everything you love, but at a price you can comfortably afford. We're going to work on getting you off of credit card dependency! It all boils down to common sense, but somehow many of us lost that along the way.

So, now that you know how a frugal lifestyle will benefit you, you can let your friends know that you're changing some aspects of how you live your life and spend your money. Hey, you just might be the

Just Remember

No matter where you're financially situated right now, you can start spending less and saving more. It starts right now. You have the power to change your spending habits, even if it seems pretty grim at the moment.

inspiration they need to take a good hard look at their own finances and make a few necessary changes themselves. Birds of a frugal feather, after all, do love to flock together.

Any change is challenging at first, and that applies to incorporating new frugal sensibilities into your life. But learning how to manage your money in a reasonable way is empow-

Learning how to manage your money in a reasonable way is empowering!

ering! And who doesn't love getting the most for their money? In the next few chapters, you'll learn how to evaluate what you really want and need so you can spend your money wisely. You will also learn some new tricks and techniques to stretch your money further while balancing your budget. You'll absolutely love it. So, get ready to explore the new, fabulous world of frugality—a place where you'll enjoy what you have, instead of longing for stuff that doesn't really matter in the first place. If you ask me, that's the truest definition of wealth I've heard.

2 | It All Begins With a Good Budget

So, you've been living the good life, have you? Buying swanky shoes or the newest technological gadget whenever the urge takes you and squandering loads of money every month on the loveliest gourmet meals your town has to offer? Maybe you got trapped in the consumerism mind-set that seemed to entitle everyone to treat himself like royalty—even if the sum total of your income was less than kingly. This chapter will help you find a new mind-set to help you save money.

It all starts with a budget. Before you freak out, remember that a budget is simply a plan for how you spend your money. I'll show you the joys (yes, it is joyful) of a budget, and you'll discover how using it keeps you firmly in control of your finances. Your budget will reveal your spending hot spots (the sidetrack spending that wastes your money) and will give you the motivation you need to change your spending ways.

Budget Necessities

You'll need these tools to help you create your budget:

Big Beautiful Budget Book–your B-4. You can use a notebook, binder or spreadsheet on your computer. Sometimes the spreadsheet is far easier to use. Use whichever system you'll find simplest *and* the one you'll use on a regular basis, period. No matter how attractive it is, it won't achieve much if it's never used. If you're using a binder, invest a few bucks in plastic inserts that will allow you to store your receipts, lists or any other bits of paperwork that you want to keep housed neatly within your budget. (If you use a spreadsheet program, then file these in an accordion-style file folder kept conveniently near your computer.)

Tracking system. A little notebook kept on hand with you all the time will not only help with tracking your actual spending (which you can later transfer into your B-4), but it can become a handy place to vent when you feel like spending! Track the purchases you made and the ones you resisted.

Filing system. This is to store records of expenses, bills, paperwork, etc. The standard rule is to keep all tax-related items (receipts from deductions, returns and copies of completed forms) for seven years. A simple way to file papers is according to category, such as Utilities, Banking, Medical, etc. At the end of the year, capture how much you spent on your utilities for the entire year, note it in your B-4 and shred the papers. You also can track these online. Export your statement as a PDF and save it in folders on your computer. You'll save trees and space in your home. Only file papers that you know you'll reference again. You'll only know what categories you need for your filing system by going through all your paperwork *first*. And remember, like a good budget, a good filing system needs to be adjusted and tweaked from time to time if you realize that it's not working as you'd hoped.

THE B-4: A BUDGET YOU CAN MANAGE

Does the idea of a budget make you break out into a cold sweat? Does it all seem too controlled for your taste? Be assured that a budget isn't about denying you happiness—far from it! A budget simply gives you important information so that you remain the master of your financial domain. A budget allows you to plan how you will use your money. Things always work better when there is a plan. You'll know at a glance how much you are spending on everything and where and when you are spending your money. It's a very empowering thing. Over time a budget will help you spend and save smarter, allowing you the freedom to make large purchases on items like furniture, vehicles or even a home of your own. These are things that you could never have purchased before, because all the sidetrack spending was keeping you down.

I call my budget the B-4—my Big Beautiful Budget Book. (I also like how it sounds because B-4 reminds me what I was like *before* I had a budget and that keeps me on track!) You can use a binder to house this foundation piece of your new lifestyle of savings or use a spreadsheet program on your computer. (I personally love the ease of the spreadsheet program, but it's completely your choice.)

Step 1: Learn Your True Income

To work out any effective budget, you first need to know what you're working with. You're going to need to figure out exactly how much income you're bringing in each month. This is simple if you are salaried or work a set number of hours each week with no variation. For people (like myself) who are freelancers, or free-spirited workers (ahem, yes free spirited, not unscheduled), this could be a bit difficult. Take your earnings from the past six months or so and come up with an average income and use this figure. (Your actual income might surprise you—you might have thought you earned a lot more, and thereby justified your overspending. Another wake up call, frugalite!)

Record how much, on average, you receive each pay period (noting the length of the pay period). Also note how much you receive, on average, each month, and finally each year. Use your tax records from the previous year to capture an accurate reflection of how much you make annually.

Your living-expense budget should be based on how much money you actually net—meaning the amount after taxes and pretax items, such as health insurance and retirement contributions, are deducted from your pay. Your net amount is the amount that you receive on your paycheck.

Your income sets the parameter for your budget. It's obvious, but if you spend more money than you earn, you'll either take on debt or eat up your savings.

Step 2: Learn Your True Spending Habits

After you've learned your true income, you need to find out exactly how you've been spending your income. Groceries vs. games, gas vs. a movie out. Those two examples show that not all budget categories are made equal. The trick to great budgeting lies in knowing what really matters in your budget and, therefore, your life. You need to decipher your budget to make it work for you, and that means plotting in the right amounts in each category and possibly even striking some of your spending altogether. And, it means learning about the three major types of expenses in your budget: fixed essentials, variable essentials and discretionary expenses.

ESSENTIAL VS. NON-ESSENTIAL EXPENSES

If you've gotten accustomed to a certain spending style, then breaking down your budget into essentials and discretionary can be a difficult task. "Yes, my video games/manicures/power tools are essential!" I can hear you say. This is where being honest with yourself comes into play in a huge way. Very few things in life are truly essential: a roof over our heads, food in our stomachs, clothing and some sort of transportation. If you need to be brutal with the budgeting, remind yourself that a lot of the pleasant extras you've been buying aren't really necessary. In fact, you might feel like your load has been lightened when you simplify your spending and your life.

Make Savings a Category

Many people find it helpful to make savings a budget category all its own. If you think of savings as just another bill to pay, it will guarantee that your savings account will continue to grow.

Three Types of Expenses

1. **Fixed essentials:** These are essential expenses that are static. Rent or mortgage payments are prime examples of this; every month you pay the same amount. Some examples of fixed essentials are:

   Mortgage or rent
   Taxes
   Insurance (home, personal and car)
   Car payments

Loan payments

Service contracts (cell phone, cable or satellite, Internet)

Home phone service

Childcare

2. **Variable essentials:** These are necessities that change in cost from month to month, such as utility bills and groceries. You can usually lower the cost in these categories, such as by shopping more carefully for groceries, using coupons, doing without or becoming energy conscious. Some examples of variable essentials are:

Utilities: water, electricity and heating costs (use your bills from the past year to come up with a monthly average)

Food: groceries

Savings

Transportation: car maintenance and repairs, car payment/lease, gas, public transportation

Clothes and shoes

Banking (includes any fees or charges; if they are too high, see about switching banks)

Haircuts

Home repairs (as needed)

Basic furnishings

Credit card payments (less use equals smaller bills)

3. **Discretionary:** After the essentials are paid for, the money left over is for discretionary use. This is for non-essentials that you still want to enjoy. Examples of discretionary items are:

Charity

Entertainment (going to the movies, renting movies, concert tickets, DVDs, albums, cover charges)

Household (home décor items, etc.)

Gym memberships

Lifestyle habits (smoking, daily coffee shop stops, etc.)

Beauty (salon/spa services, cosmetics)

Food (dining out)

Gifts

Spending money (when you use the Grown-Up Allowance Plan, you'll want to track what you've given yourself as spending money [see below])

Vacation fund

Customize categories (you need to account for every dollar you spend, so create custom categories for your budget as needed)

Armed with this knowledge, you can now begin to evaluate your spending patterns. Take out all of your old bills, receipts and

The Grown-Up Allowance Plan

The Grown-Up Allowance Plan is simply the money you give yourself for silly spending. My husband and I allow twenty dollars per person per week, and we track this total amount in our budget under Spending Money. While we track the amount, we don't need to keep track of how we specifically spent this money, which gives me freedom to buy a few little extras—like a gooey goodie at the bakery, a new lipstick, or a paperback book—just because I want them. If your budget allows for this, you might also find this helpful! Generally, a budget that is overly strict is one that won't be adhered to for very long.

bank statements from at least the past six months. Record all your expenses, breaking them down into the categories of fixed essentials, variable essentials and discretionary. It's trickier if you've been paying cash and don't have a lot of receipts, but you'll be able to patch together the facts you need. Do it now. By the end of this, you should have a complete list of all the outgoing expenditures you have every month, plus a list of all your debt. (We'll discuss how to tackle that debt in chapter three). The easiest way to do this is to create one spreadsheet (or sheet in your notebook) for each month you are tracking. Then create three separate list of fixed essentials, variable essentials and discretionary for each month. When you are done, you should be able to quickly tally each type of expense for each month. Use these totals to come up with a monthly average for your variable essentials and your discretionary spending. Your fixed expenses should be the same each month.

To figure out your budget, follow these simple steps:

1. Deduct your monthly fixed essential expenses from your true income for the month. Write down the figure you're left with.

2. Deduct the average of your variable essential expenses from the figure you were left with at the end of step 1. This leaves you with your discretionary expenses amount.

3. Take the amount you are left with at the end of step 2 and compare it with the list of discretionary (non-essential) expenses you have. Play with the numbers to try to make the money and the expenses fit. Keep in mind that to create a balanced budget, you'll likely need to reduce your costs on variable essential *and* be willing to sacrifice a few discretionary expenses. Your goal is to break even at the end of the month. Leftover money can go into savings. A negative

amount at the end of the month means you either dipped into your savings or added to your debt load.

What were the results of tracking your past expenses? Scary, or not as bad as you expected? Regardless of what your paperwork showed, you now need to plan to make changes, especially if you're in a deficit situation at the end of the month! With a highlighter, mark every single variable essential and discretionary expense that you can reduce. In each of these, make a goal of what you want to save and write specifically how you're going to do it.

You can't do much about some fixed expenses, but if you're not bound by a contract, or your contract is almost up, see what you can do to tackle each one to lower costs dramatically each month. Check around and compare Internet providers and see what special rates are going on right now, and then switch. Do the same for electric providers, phone companies, etc., if this is possible in your area. Impressive savings can also add up by bundling—a technique that companies use to give you a bargain when you utilize more than one of their products or services. If you can save $100 a month on utilities, that is after-tax money that can go directly onto your debt repayment or into your savings account or investments. An extra $1,200 bucks a year is certainly nothing to sneeze at, frugalite!

These changes will only happen when you make them happen. No more victimization here, please! You can take this battle back into your hands again. You'll find recommendations to lower each variable expense in the different chapters of this book. Plus, you'll start keeping track of exactly where and when you spend your money, which will give you the data needed to keep making positive changes.

Once you've seen what you are actually spending on variables, decide what you want to be spending on them. Use the monthly figures to find averages for your grocery bill, transportation and other variables. Is one category going to eat up most of your money? That's a prime category to make some changes and cutbacks. Come up with a realistic amount you can spend monthly for each category. That is your new budget. Aim to spend only that much money on that category that month. This sets boundaries on your spending and helps you make the best choices with your money.

TRACK YOUR SPENDING

For a budget to be its most effective, you need to track every single penny that leaves your pocket. Some of my friends who watch me do this think I'm a little extreme. Even on vacation, I take a mini, spiral-bound notebook and track all of my spending, keeping to a preset —and reasonable—budget. Okay, so it might seem nerdy, and you might get teased a little at first, but once you start bragging about the credit card bill you paid off and the new sofa that you saved up and paid for with cash, your pals will start asking for advice, which you can confidently and humbly provide.

Daily Spending

To help you track, at the very front of your B-4, place some lined sheets for what I call "Daily Spending." (For spreadsheet users, create a new page with that title.) This is where you'll track your day-to-day spending. You'll need columns for the date, items purchased, amount spent and category this expense will be placed in. Then make good use of these pages by filling them in whenever you spend money. The easiest way to do this is to keep all your receipts (even for cash purchases) and input them at the end of every week (daily if you shop a lot). If you do this every week, it will only take ten to fifteen minutes to update the sheet. You can do it during a commercial break of your favorite TV show. At the end of the month, you'll tally up all spending in each category and add it to your monthly overview pages.

Monthly Overview

The monthly overview pages go in the second section of your B-4. They let you see, on a monthly basis, where your money is going. Use one page per month of the year, so you can quickly see where exactly you spent your hard-earned money. List all major categories and the totals tallied from your Daily Spending pages to get amounts.

At the end of the first month, evaluate how you did. Don't get frustrated if your budget doesn't work perfectly the first month, as it truly is a work in progress. When you see that $200 just wasn't a reasonable amount for groceries (especially if your goal is to eat at home more), you can tweak that by taking from another category and see if $250 will work for you. A good budget is flexible, not forced, so readjust as needed to create a tailored budget that fits you as perfectly as a pair of trousers.

Budget Journaling

The third section (or new spreadsheet) in your B-4 is a journal where you can occasionally track how you're doing, what you saved on, what you feel you overspent on and how your progress is coming along overall.

Note major, unexpected expenses here, like an auto or home repair or a medical emergency. Also write goals here. If you want to save for a vacation or a new couch or a new car, write that down. If you're in the market for a big ticket item, start writing down prices from different stores so you can be sure you get the best deal. Tracking prices will also help you know when an item is truly on sale.

You also can use this as an emotional release—where you get to write how you feel about this new plan, any obstacles encountered along the way and the progress you're making. If you're not big into writing, you can just jot down a few notes now and again that relate directly to the facts. No pressure. Make this area work for you.

FIND YOUR MONEY SPENDING HOT SPOTS

This part might get a little bit painful: It's time to get completely honest with yourself and deal with how you're spending your money. When you created your budget, you used your bank and credit card statements and receipts to track where your money went. Use that information to see where your spending hot spots are. Your spending hot spots are the products or services that you spend the most money on, those that you find difficult to resist. For some it's travel, for some it's fashion and for others it's computers and gadgets.

Remind Yourself Why You're Doing This

Write a note to remind yourself *why* you're determined to be financially responsible and post it in your B-4, on your refrigerator or taped onto the computer screen. Go on, write it. I'm saving money because: "I want to be in control of my money for once!" or "I want to go to Tahiti and sip fruity drinks by the sea!" or "I want to pay off that horrible student loan!" Keep it in a prominent spot, where you'll see it when tempting spending situations arise.

Once you find these hot spots, you can work on dousing the fire. No matter what it is you're currently overspending on, you can stop those spending patterns immediately, turn around and control your finances. The first step is awareness.

The four major categories we'll discuss in this book are Home and Living; Food; Entertainment, Celebrations and Vacations; and Beauty and Style. This is certainly not an exhaustive list, but by managing all of these areas, it will dramatically change your money situation for the better. I like to call these big categories the Four Biggies of Family Finance. Whew, try saying that four times in a row. Each category has its own chapter full of ways to save. For now, here's a quick overview to help you with your budget.

1. **Home and Living:** These are some of the biggest, baddest expenses in your budget and include rent or mortgage, utilities, upkeep costs, home furnishings and electronic gadgets, banking fees, maintenance charges and vehicle costs. This is also the area to track your debt. As a kickstart to savings, write down the areas in this section that you can reduce:

   _____

   _____

   _____

   _____

2. **Food:** Probably the single largest variable expense in your budget, food includes not only groceries but also anything that you consume away from home. This includes eating out at restaurants or fast-food joints, coffee runs and snacks from the convenience store or gas station. It's time to get honest about which of these are spending hot spots for you:

_____

_____

_____

_____

3. **Entertainment, Celebrations and Vacations:** Gifts add up, as do all of those nights out with friends (not to mention the movies you love to rent and your huge music collection). Figure out how to give thoughtful gifts and have a good time without breaking your budget. Traveling is a great way to relax and gain meaningful life experiences. Figure out a way to jet-set without obliterating your savings account. Note where you spend too much in these areas:

_____

_____

_____

_____

Housing: 35 Percent and Under

When it comes to housing costs—which is the biggie in our budget, usually the very largest cost—your aim should be to spend no more than 35 percent of your net income on housing and associated costs. Spending too much? Aim to lower costs by taking on a roommate, moving to a cheaper apartment or refinancing your mortgage, or else you might have to slash your budget in other ways to allow for your pricey housing situation.

4. **Beauty and Style:** Everything that goes on you to make you look great is counted right here. That means clothing, accessories, haircuts, gym memberships, makeup, beauty and skin care, and salon and spa treatments. Okay, fess up, and jot down the things you spend too much on to beautify your already oh-so beautiful self:

_____

_____

_____

_____

There are obviously other places where your money can be spent, but these four major areas, once under control, will contribute to a much greater sense of financial peace. If you know of another area where you're spending too much, well, you're not off the hook. You're the only one who can change your financial situation. A good budget, after all, is as flexible as any Pilates instructor. And, any good budget is completely personalized, meaning it will take some time, effort and adjusting to get it just right for you and your personal circumstances.

Once you know the what and where of your cash expenditures, you can begin to unravel the why, as in: "Why do you spend?" Only you can discover your emotional triggers for shopping. For some of us, it's to relieve feelings of tension when we've had a particularly taxing day at work. Others use it as a reward for a job well done. For others it goes deeper. Some people believe their worth as a person is expressed in material things. Some people get a self-esteem boost when they buy the latest gadget or hottest fashion trend. The next time you're tempted to shop without a purpose, ask yourself: "Why do I want to shop right now? Will it really help me in the long term?" Be honest with yourself and identify your own reasons for emotional shopping, or shopping without a purpose. It might be a very revealing exercise and help aid you to control impulse shopping. Don't be afraid to confront your true feelings, and if you discover you need help with your self-esteem, get it. You are worth far more than anything you could ever own, and you don't need stuff to prove your value.

HOW TO SHOP ON A BUDGET

You've created your B-4 and identified your spending hot spots. Fantastic! Now comes the really important part—actually using your budget in your daily life! Let's discover how your newly created B-4 will become useful to you as you live and breathe your new frugal life.

The Cash Payment Method

Some people become more aware of their true spending when they see the cash go out in a very literal way—by putting the budgeted cash into jars or envelopes at the beginning of each week and then taking out the cash they need for every purchase. Got seventy-five dollars for groceries this week? Then pop that exact amount into the "food" jar or envelope on Monday, and that's what you've got for groceries until you refill your cash jar (which won't be until next week).

If using any cards (credit or debit) without losing control is a struggle, you should try the cash-only method. It might be just the jolt you need to sit up and take notice of your real spending habits. Leave your cards and checkbook at home when you go shopping and only take cash. You will be forced to stick to your budget.

Shopaholic Warning: BYB

This has absolutely nothing to do with bringing your own booze, I promise you. It has everything to do with budget consciousness. If you have a tendency to go a bit nuts whenever a shopping opportunity strikes, remember one catchy little motto: BYB, which stands for *beyond your budget*. Translation? No bargain is a bargain if you can't afford it! It doesn't matter how cute those wedge shoes are or how adorable those hanging earrings would look with that floral dress. If your bank account or your wallet can't cover the cost, then it's beyond your budget. BYB. I sing this to myself to the tune of Michael Jackson's *P.Y.T.* (Pretty Young Thing). Has a real ring to it, doesn't it? Keep it in mind as you work to stay within your allotted budget.

To stick to your budget, you'll need to shop with a purpose. The kids need new jeans? Great, you've got your purpose in mind and a list detailing exactly what you need to buy. But a list alone won't help if you haven't checked to see that it works within your budget, so before doing anything else, check your B-4 budget to see where things stand. How much do you reasonably have to spend on clothing this month? What can you spend on those jeans? On the list, write out the maximum amount you can spend and then stick to that shopping budget. Get accustomed to never leaving home without it—a budget-adhering list, that is.

> No bargain is a bargain if you just can't afford it!

Keeping a notebook or journal with you all the time will really help when you're tempted to spend on an impulse purchase. First, remove yourself from the situation by walking out of the store. Just put that item down and walk away. I promise that it won't kill you. Second, take out your notebook or laptop—whatever you use to track purchases—and write down the details of the incident. Why did you want to buy? (Be honest with yourself here. Was it because work is particularly stressful today? Or, you're just feeling a bit sad? Write down the real reason, and it'll help you learn more about why you buy.) What was the item? What was the price? How did you manage to walk away with empty hands and a heavier wallet? These little victories will give you confidence later when you face temptation again. On the other hand, if you didn't succeed and ended up buying the item, once you journal about it, you'll likely want to take it back for a refund if it was an impulse buy—a want, not a need.

Credit Card Cry-Out

Write down on a sticky note your current debt level and place this reminder right on any credit card or debit card you use. This strong dose of reality will slap you in the face at any impulsive moment.

Resisting Impulse Buys

We've all been caught in the impulse buy trap. Whether it was a lipstick that looked gorgeous under those store lights (but oh so wrong on your lips out in daylight) or a "handy" gadget (that didn't work like you thought it would and so never saw the light of day again), we've all been ensnared. So, when you're caught in the high emotion of the moment, do the following:

1. **Discover your triggers to buy.** Maybe it's a stressful day of work that makes you want to shop. Emotional shopping is much like emotional eating. When you know your triggers, find another way to release pent up stress besides shopping.

2. **Shop on an even keel.** Research shows that both really good moods and really bad moods can increase impulse buying. So, when possible, shop when you feel balanced … you won't be as likely to indulge.

3. **Ask yourself why it seems so important to have this thing.** Does it matter more than getting your debt reduced or helping to save for retirement?

4. **Just walk away.** If you're absolutely gone for it, ask the sales-person to hold the item for you for a day. If after a day you realize you don't need it, then you're victorious!

Once the money for any one category is gone for that month—let's say for clothing—then stop shopping for that category! Don't tempt yourself needlessly by going to the mall. Instead, find other free things to do with your time. See chapter seven for lots of ideas on free or low-cost activities that will keep you away from the mall. When the money for the month is gone, it is quite simply gone. So, to stick to your budget, and don't torture yourself when you haven't a penny more to spend.

SPENDING CHALLENGE

To get into the spirit of saving money right now, try this challenge as soon as you can. Here's your first spending challenge: No-Spend Days. It's all those little things that you spend your money on that add up, things that a week or two later you can't even remember. You know what I mean, the pack of gum and chocolate bar at the gas station, the pumped up latte to go, the fast-food lunches. All you remember is seeing the drain loosened on your debit account! So,

Department Store Cards

A shiny little booth beckoned you, and before you knew it, the clever salesperson had convinced you that you needed that store card. Sure, they come complete with some pretty helpful incentives—20 percent off your first purchase and special packets of coupons mailed to you throughout the year. But, department store cards can come back to bite you—particularly with interest charges. Some of these cards can top 29 percent interest rates! So, unless you're incredibly disciplined and can use these cards for the benefits alone and then pay off the balance in full, it's best to pass these by.

challenge yourself to a No-Spend Day—and do it often. Plan ahead to make this goal doable. Take a thermos of coffee to work with you if stopping for coffee is a major challenge. Tote your lunch to work along with snacks if eating out is your culprit. Or browse the Internet at lunch or lounge in the sunshine outside instead of heading to the shops to spend. In the journal section of your B-4, keep track of when you did this challenge and how you made out. A No-Spend Day challenge is a fantastic one for making you stand up and take notice of how much money you've really been wasting on random junk.

A budgeted life is an altogether better life! Keeping track of the money that goes in and out of your household will mean you're in control once and for all. Budgeting can seem intimidating, particularly if you've never tried it before. But, it's so easy to get hooked on the helpfulness of this practice, especially after you see your money stretching further, and you can add more money to your savings account. You'll be so glad that you made the effort to change.

3 | Defeating Debt

Debt is a four-letter word in all of the nastiest ways. Living with debt can literally affect your health. Worrying about how to pay back money may make sleep nearly impossible. You can become anxious, distracted and mentally or emotionally overwhelmed. The constant, nagging concern about what you owe can make your stomach clench and your muscles and head ache, or you might even develop an unwanted worry partner in your gut—a burning ulcer. All told, debt is no joke; it is agonizing. But, no matter what your situation is, you can successfully haul yourself back out of the pit of debt. We're going to get you started in this chapter. And believe me, the very act of acknowledging the problem and working on it will alleviate much of the anxiety and feelings of helplessness you've been enduring.

At first, the scariest part of facing your finances is realizing the depth of your debt load. It'll feel like looking at a monster eye to eye. You see, many of us are masterful debt deniers. While we might worry in a general way about our debt, we stick our heads in the sand

and refuse to open those scary "past due" statements and ignore the phone calls from creditors. And, ironically, some of us find that one way to ease the feelings of despair is to go shopping. Shopping! Which only makes the situation worse, of course, but at the time, a little retail therapy feels quite comforting indeed.

Okay, so let's get honest about our debt now. This will undoubtedly make you feel a little squeamish, but rest assured that it makes everyone feel that way at first. Later on, you'll come to recognize that facing these truths can empower you to make serious changes that will relieve your stress and anxiety because you're battling the very source of the distress.

HOW TO USE—NOT ABUSE—CREDIT CARDS

Credit cards are wonderfully helpful, in theory. The problem is that, over the past couple of decades, many people forgot what using a credit card really meant—that you are basically borrowing money to purchase something that you can't otherwise afford. We'd forgotten common sense: In order to buy something we want, we need to save up our money for it instead of relying on borrowing more credit. Credit became easier and easier to get and was easily accessible via those pretty and colorful cards in our wallets.

This is not to say that all credit card usage is bad or wrong. In fact, using credit cards wisely improves your credit rating, which means you'll be entitled to lower interest rates on large loans and mortgages. And they're necessary tools for booking hotel rooms or rental cars when you're planning a vacation. Using credit cards isn't the problem; overusing them is. This dependency on credit has become epidemic as people reach for credit to pay for even their day-to-day necessities like groceries or gas.

CREDIT CARD DOS AND DON'TS

Do

- Use credit cards occasionally, and then aim to pay off the total right away. This helps build good credit, as it proves that you use credit wisely.
- Remember that anything purchased on credit cards isn't really yours until you've paid off the amount in full. It's like taking out a mortgage on that sofa—wouldn't you rather just save for it and buy it outright?
- Shop around for the best interest rates. The lower, the better.
- Call your own credit provider and ask for a lower interest rate. If you have a good history with them, and you explain that you've been offered lower rates elsewhere, they may be happy to lower your rate to retain your account.

Don't

- Have more than two or three credit cards. It becomes a confusing mess and increases your chances of having a heavy load of debt. The more cards you have, the more likely you'll overuse them.
- Apply for cards too often. Each application for new credit is noted on your credit report and counts against your rating. Plus, it doesn't look good if you've applied for a bunch of cards in a short period of time—it makes you look financially desperate and risky.
- Get suckered into accepting department store cards you really don't need. Those are the ones with the jaw-dropping interest rates that can reach nearly 30 percent!
- Pay for everyday purchases with credit. Budget properly and

pay with cash for things like groceries, gas and even clothing. It might mean you have to wait a while before getting that new dress you love, but at least when you buy it you've truly *bought* it, not just loaned it.

- Get swayed by the dizzying variety of bonuses and rewards that come with certain cards. Mileage points and rewards are great, but paying through the nose with much higher interest rates doesn't do any good to anyone but the issuing bank. Many people use these bonuses to justify making everyday purchases with a credit card. Even if you intend to pay off the balance every month, it's very easy to lose track of how much you spend. Know your limitations. If you're a person who doesn't keep close track of your spending, pay with cash only.

- Make only minimum payments. It'll take you years to pay off

How to Stop Reaching for a Card

It's all in changing habits. Have you become accustomed to grabbing a credit card to pay for most anything? Keep cards at home if you can't stop spending with them, and use cash instead. Paying with cash forces you to stay on budget. Here's a downright chilly trick: Place your credit card in a container of water and freeze it. If the shopping bug bites, you'll have to wait for your credit card ice cubes to thaw, and by that time you'll likely have come to your senses. Freezing shouldn't damage the magnetic strip on the card, which is very tough and not affected by temperature changes. But, you'll have to let the card thaw au naturel. Using the microwave will damage the magnetic strip on the card, making it unusable.

a balance if you stick to minimums. The only time it makes sense to pay a minimum is when you've chosen another credit card or bill to pay as your focus bill and you're maintaining lower payments on all the other bills.

- Just close out that credit card. Check the fine print first because closing out certain cards will negatively impact your credit rating. If your card has a balance, you should never just close the card out. The balance won't be closed along with it. Your oldest credit card should usually be kept open because it provides you with a longer history of credit, which is beneficial to your credit health.

DEVISE A "DEFEAT THE DEBT" PLAN

Facing your debt means gathering all of the necessary facts together. Yes, it means opening those dastardly bills you might have been hiding from. You will create lists of both your basic expenses like mortgage/rent, food, childcare and gas, and also a listing of every debt you have. You'll calculate your true income and list your assets to see where you really stand. This will be a snap if you've already followed the B-4 plan in chapter two.

Get out a sheet of paper and put a bold title across the top that shows you mean business: "My Defeat the Debt Plan." This document will show you where your money has been going and, with some work, where that money can be more cleverly used to pay off your debt faster. The very title is empowering, making us realize that we are the only ones who can go out and battle our debt. No more victimization here, folks, because we got ourselves into this mess in the first place. It's time to own up to it, face it and then go after it! We're going to destroy this debt once and for all.

It's the "Defeat the Debt Plan," and it boils down to four basic steps:

1. Find out your financial numbers. These are your income, expenses, debt and assets.
2. Cut back on all possible expenses to contribute more towards your debt repayment plan.
3. Decide the order of debt repayment.
4. Implement the plan. This is when you put your money where your mouth is, or where your bills are, and make changes to how you spend, pay and save.

Facing your debt means gathering all of the necessary facts. It means opening those dastardly bills you might have been hiding from.

There might be only four steps involved, but each step involves a lot of work and changing some old habits. You might have gotten pretty comfortable with those habits over the years, but if you take a hard look at them, you'll see that they've done you no good. These new habits will change up the routine and get you started towards debt freedom.

Your Financial Numbers

Step 1: Income. First, you need to know what you're working with in terms of income—how much money you really bring in every month. At the top of the first page, list the after-tax (net) income in your household. Include every source of income, even small amounts of extra earnings from activities like selling Avon or holding garage sales, or larger amounts, such as money collected from rental properties you own. If the number is lower than you thought and you'd like to increase it, look to the end of this chapter for twenty ways to make extra income.

Step 2: Expenses. Second comes the listing of expenses—shelter (rent or mortgage; your mortgage being one of the only categories which will be listed under necessities and debt), utilities, taxes, phone, Internet, groceries, clothes, childcare, insurance, etc. This should be an exhaustive list, including anything and everything that you regularly spend money on. Your B-4 should already have everything accounted for. Simply add up your fixed, variable and discretionary expenses to get an expenses total. On your original "Defeat the Debt" page, note your expenses below your income.

Step 3: Debts. List all of your debts, such as credit cards, loans and lines of credit. No matter how ugly, you need to open all your bank statements, credit card statements and invoices to see what you really owe. Note in brackets beside each amount the interest rates you're currently paying and what the minimum monthly payment is. If you've borrowed any money from friends and family, then include these "creditors" on your debt list. Add all of your debt together for your total debt. You might be shocked by this number, but that horror might be exactly the motivation you need to stop overspending and commit yourself to defeating debt.

Step 4: Assets. Finally, list any assets you have, such as properties or vehicles or artwork. If debt becomes too devastating, selling an asset can provide you with an easier way back to solvency. List any investments, savings accounts, retirement savings accounts, etc.

Now, you have a clearer picture of your financial situation. Sure, it might not be the prettiest picture at the moment, but over time, this information will help get you out of debt. So, be grateful for it. You've taken the first step out of the hole, which is often the hardest.

A Grown-Up Report Card: Credit Reports

Credit reports are valuable sources of information and are relied on by banks and other financial institutions to check your financial standing when you want to take out a loan or get a new credit card. Sometimes, even employers or potential landlords will access this information. According to a 2004 federal law, everyone can receive a free credit report once per year via the mail from any of the three credit reporting agencies: Equifax, TransUnion or Experian. If you want to access your report immediately, you'll have to pay. (In Canada, TransUnion and Equifax work the same way; you can get a free report by post or pay fifteen to twenty-five dollars for immediate access online.) Check your credit report for any discrepancies and report them immediately.

Now that you have some financial facts at hand, get to work using these numbers to your benefit.

Plunk your own numbers into the following formula:

INCOME – EXPENSES = Money to pay off debt

Let's say you have $3,400 of monthly income minus $3,000 of expenses (which includes the minimum monthly payment for each debt). You're left with $400 for additional debt repayment. That's *before* we get out our red marker to slash expenses!

Cut Back on Expenses

Whether or not there's money left over for debt repayment, each expense should be scrutinized to see how you can cut back on your

Selling Assets

If the situation is dire, consider selling an asset, whether it's your home, a vehicle or an investment. For many people in debt, selling an asset to unload the debt may be well worth the sacrifice. This isn't a decision to be made lightly, so always talk it over with your family and professionals first.

spending. This will leave you with more money to pay down your debt, or in the case of not having any money for debt repayment, it'll mean you forage to find some. Most of the chapters in this book are filled with ideas for spending less on the necessities and niceties of life. Use a red marker or pen to mark the expenses you can slash. On a separate page, brainstorm all the ideas you can think of to make this savings happen.

Once you've started to save on expenses, rework your debt formula, which might now look like this:

Income $3,400 – Expenses $2,700 = $700
That extra money goes to pay down your debt.

When you know how much you have to put towards debt repayment, you can plan your first *focus bill*.

Decide the Order of Debt Repayment

Focus bills are simply the ones you're focusing on right now to pay off quickly. They aren't randomly selected, but are chosen according to one of two variables: the amount owing or the interest accruing.

If you have a tiny bill that you can pay off in just a month or two, it's beneficial to do so. It gets your debt destruction off to a roaring start and gives you a psychological boost. Otherwise, select the bill with the highest interest rate as your first focus bill. Focus more of your resources and attention on one bill at a time, to get it paid off quickly. Extra earnings should go towards paying this focus bill, and generally the higher interest debts are the ones that should be paid off first. This makes sense because you'll be paying less and less interest as you attack that principle. Remember to maintain at least the minimum payments on all your debts as you do the focus bill payments. Once you pay off bill A, the amount you used to pay on that bill will go towards bill B, along with the minimum you were paying on bill B to start with. Bill B becomes your new focus bill. Using this technique (which many call "snowballing") will get your debts paid off faster than you ever imagined.

A Word About Savings

Some say that beyond a basic savings account with a thousand bucks or so for emergencies, that there's no need to save until after your debt is cleared. But without a savings cushion, you'll likely end up back in debt again when the unexpected strikes (such as medical expenses or car repairs) and you are forced to reach for your credit cards again. That's why any debt destruction plan should also include savings. A thousand bucks won't go far in a real emergency, so make it your aim to add "savings" to your list of expenses every month. That's one expense that *should* increase with time!

Implement the Plan

All the planning in the world won't do any good if you don't dig down and *implement* the plan, or put it into action. Making these changes takes a lot of determination; no one else can change your financial situation except you.

Implement the plan to destroy debt by:

- Tracking everything you spend and making a conscious effort to spend less. (Sometimes, that simply means staying away from the stores when you don't have extra cash to spend.) Keeping a notebook or electronic device handy all the time will help you to see where your money is really going. Tracking it can help you stop overspending.

- Refusing to get back into your old destructive habits of credit card dependency. Give yourself a "cooling off period" before any major purchase with credit. Go home and write down why you wanted the item so badly and whether or not you really need it. If you've purchased something impulsively you can always return it!

Time to Call in the Pros

If you've done the research and are trying to control your debt and yet still find that you're struggling, it might be time to seek professional guidance. Nonprofit organizations provide debt counseling to consumers in over their heads. Check with the Better Business Bureau to ensure that the organization is qualified to help. Sometimes, bankruptcy might be the only course of action if you've gotten in too deep.

- Re-read this chapter as many times as it takes to stay focused on your ultimate goals.
- Read blogs and Web sites of people who *have* successfully dug themselves out of debt. Some people have paid off $100,000 or more of consumer debt alone! Going to the library is also a great way to find new resources on how to save money and how others have faced off against debt and come out victorious.

Finally, just *start*. Get your personal financial worksheet completed and then start making all the changes you possibly can. At first, it'll all feel very new and uncomfortable, but by the end of the first week, when you see you still have money left over, you'll get into the groove of this money awareness game.

These techniques—applied over and over, month after month—will keep working to lower your overall debt, until finally, one beautiful day, you can celebrate and have a huge "Say Goodbye to Debt" party! And yes, I'd love an invitation, thank you.

IDEAS FOR INCREASING YOUR INCOME TO PAY DEBT

Once you have your income and expense documents completed, you'll see that adding more income to your household will help make ends meet *and* will allow you to pay off your debt faster. Be determined that any extra money earned goes directly towards debt. This isn't extra spending money to go crazy with, so remain focused on your goal. Even five or ten extra bucks here and there works toward the cause; all of those small amounts really add up impressively. Keeping track of every debt you pay off helps keep you motivated, so, just like with your B-4 budget, keep track of your extra income that you've used to pay off debt.

Twenty Ways to Increase Income

With debt repayment firmly in mind, here are twenty ways to bring extra cash into your household:

1. **Take on a few extra shifts at work.** Ask around to see if anyone needs a shift covered, or go right to the source and ask your employer if it's possible to take on extra work. Sometimes just posting a note on the coffee room bulletin board will yield great results.

2. **Pick up a part-time job.** Ask around and see if friends or family know who's hiring in your area.

3. **Sell stuff.** If you don't need it, don't hold on to it. The extra cash earned can reduce your debt dramatically, which is more valuable to your peace of mind than an old vehicle sitting in the garage or an old sofa gathering dust. Make a list of things you could sell. You might be able to knock off one debt entirely from this tip alone!

4. **Sell stuff in an organized way.** Home parties or home selling via catalogue (like with Avon) is a great way to make some extra money. Choose a program that has no or limited start-up costs, so that if it's not right for you, you haven't lost money. Ask others who have worked the program for their honest feedback.

> ## Decrease to Increase
>
> Keep in mind that the no. 1 way to *increase* your income is to *decrease* your spending! That's where the startling red pen comes in handy, slashing your outgoing expenditures.

5. **Mystery shopping.** Making money simply by shopping or eating at restaurants undercover sounds like a dream job, but there really are people who get paid to do just this. Keep in mind, however, that legitimate mystery shopping organizations will *never* ask you to pay to get assignments. If they ask you to pay, run the other way.

6. **Freelance writing.** If you have a knack with the written word, use it to your advantage. Writing-market guides have listings of Web sites and magazines looking to pay writers for content. Or, try blogging online and adding pay-per-click advertising (such as Google AdSense) and build your blog community. Successful bloggers can make a full-time income from their blogs!

7. **Pet services.** You can be hired for dog walking, pet sitting, even puppy poop scooping! There are always people willing to pay for you to help them kindly care for their pets.

8. **Housecleaning.** It's easy to find housecleaning jobs if you're willing to do a little legwork. Create some fliers on your computer and slide them under doors in your neighborhood or condo complex. Research to see what the going rates are in your area.

9. **Sell your knowledge.** If you're a whiz on the computer, teach classes to newbies. If you're an accomplished artist, teach classes in that. Use your skills to pay those bills!

10. **Tutoring.** If you're qualified to teach professionally, tutor in your spare time. It can pay very well and be very fulfilling.

11. **Handyman services.** Even better if you come complete with a truck! It's incredible what a small classified ad will yield, so give it a try and turn yourself into a Mr. or Ms. Fix-It.

12. **Consignment clothing.** Your old clothes can be an extra pay-check waiting to happen! If your clothes are in good condition, you can sell them on consignment to stores in your area. Some people find treasures for just a dollar or two at the thrift store and then resell them and make a nice profit at chic consignment stores.

13. **Create a local Web site.** Whether it's a directory or classified ads, creating a local site can earn you advertising revenue. Do your research first to see what your area is lacking online: a tourist site, a business directory, a listing of apartments for rent, etc.

14. **Rent out some space.** It could be in your garage or a basement suite or a room in your home.

15. **Painting and decorating.** Are you a decorating diva just waiting to be discovered? Word of mouth may be all it takes—help out a friend, and then ask him to tell other friends and so on.

16. **Antique-wise: Buy and resell online at eBay.** Just be sure you've properly researched the items and know you are getting the real thing. Also, only buy the item if you are 100% positive you can sell it for more than you pay for it.

17. **Cleaning computers (inside and out).** Computer keyboards are teeming with microscopic little critters that can make us sick. And the interior of our computers can become tainted and slow. If you know how, cleaning computers inside and out can become a successful way to earn cash.

18. **Bake a cake.** Or "butter up" your co-workers by bringing in your famous squares and cookies one day a week, but for a price. If you're an amazing baker, then word will get around.

Some home businesses have started in just this way because most of us can't resist a delicious homemade snack.

19. **Garage sale.** Up the income potential by offering icy cold drinks in the summer or hot cocoa in the winter. As far as your inventory goes, make sure you're not selling anything valuable for pennies. Check eBay if you're curious about a certain item's collectable value.

20. **Discover lost money**. I saved the coolest one for last. There are thousands of savings bonds and bank accounts with people's names on them that sit unclaimed for years. Do a search to see if you happen to have just such an account. Be sure to search using your full legal name, any nicknames or other versions of your name that you go by and any previous surnames you may have. If your search turns up some lost money, fill out any paperwork required to claim the cash and sit back and wait for a check to appear.

4 Saving Is a Family Affair

As you continue your travels along this lovely road towards big savings, you'll notice that you're not the only traveler. Who's that cute little person over there? Isn't that someone you (or your beloved) just happened to give birth to? And who's that hunk of manhood, or gorgeous specimen of womanhood moseying along? Lucky you, it's your significant other! You'll need your family to join in on this journey of savings with you if you want to reach your financial goals. That's why this chapter is devoted to helping you get your family involved in your new living large on less plan. And, although pets can't help you save money, we'll also touch on how you can save on the essentials needed to keep your feathered, furry or finned friends happy and healthy, too.

WORKING AS A TEAM FOR SAVINGS

Remember how Mary Poppins could turn anything—even a spoonful of vile medicine—into a wonderful game? Keep her strategy firmly in mind when you're establishing new saving habits for your family. How so? Make everything frugal a fantastic game and you'll have happy new frugalites hatching in your nest before you know it. Plus, as a bonus, you'll also be teaching your family that financial responsibility doesn't always have to be a chore—it's a necessity, but one that reaps huge dividends.

The Plan

Good intentions don't equal good results unless you have a plan of action to help you get there. A goal without a plan is like a meal without utensils—it might look temptingly good, but there's no way to get in there and enjoy all the benefits of what's set before you. Your family needs to know about this plan to save money in order for it to work.

You need to communicate to your family three basic aspects of your new spending patterns right from the outset:

1. **Why** you need to change your spending patterns as a family. Give as much information as is necessary. If your situation is dire, there's no need to scare everyone. Also, only provide information that kids can understand and won't be overwhelmed by. (Age appropriate information is important. Young children will only need to know that Mom and Dad want to save more money or pay off a few bills. Older kids can know more details if you're comfortable sharing them.)

2. **What** your current spending patterns have been. Armed with facts and figures from your B-4 budget (see chapter two), you can shed light on what's been good and bad about how the family has been spending money. Don't point fingers of blame at anyone; work at this as a team from the beginning to encourage your family to change for all the right reasons.

3. **How** you're going to change. The way you spend—and account for that spending—as a family is going to completely change. Be as specific as possible, again taking into account the age of your children and what information they can readily digest. Get feedback from your family members. You'll be amazed by how their input and involvement will change new budgeting habits into something the whole family considers a challenge to undertake instead of a burden. This is your plan for action, including spending challenges, budgets, etc. You'll create goals, such as saving for the kids' education or paying off a car loan, and create charts and progress reports so that family members can see at a glance how their work is paying off.

Families who are happily living large on less do one thing really well: communicate. They make goals as a family, then track their progress and talk about what went right and wrong along the way. They don't blame each other for their current financial situation, but rather go at this savings challenge as a team, all in it together. If your family doesn't consist of natural communicators, perhaps especially not about money, then some habits are going to have to change. In fact, budget consciousness may very well open more lines of communication within your family. Set a day each week to discuss how everyone did with the budget during the past week and to stay focused on longer-term goals, such as savings. Young children may not have much to contribute to the meeting, but this is a great time to update everyone on the progress you are making toward your goals. Kids can stay for the update and then you and your spouse can discuss spending in detail after you let the kids leave the meeting.

THE REAL COST OF A TWO-INCOME FAMILY

Two incomes don't necessarily mean a larger bank account for the family when you consider additional costs associated with full-time work. To gauge if one of your incomes is helping your family's bottom line, take your income and then subtract the following costs to see what you're really bringing home each month.

- **Childcare costs.** This one is a biggie. Childcare costs constitute the largest spending category for working parents. If you'd like an alternative to daycare, make a list of people you trust to take care of your children and approach them with a plan to see if they could care for your kids. Or approach your employer to see if options such as flexible schedules, telecommuting or job sharing are available. If flexible schedules are possible, try to overlap your spouse's schedule and yours as much as possible, so childcare costs are kept at a minimum.

Tracking Your Success

No matter what financial challenge your family works on first, you need to track your progress and success along the way. Trying to save for a fun family adventure to a theme park? Do like any good fundraiser would do and motivate your troops with an oversized savings thermometer—the "temperature" goes up and up as the money does, and the kids can also help contribute to the total. Or, in the case of debt repayment, do a reverse thermometer where you can white out the debt as it goes down, edging ever closer to that beautiful zero mark.

Unless your job pays well, childcare costs alone might prevent you from returning to work full-time.

- **Clothing costs.** If you're working in any sort of office environment, the price of clothing will be higher compared to more casual work, but you can save by utilizing the money saving tips in chapter eight.
- **Dining out and lunches.** Try your best to brown-bag and take last night's leftovers for lunch if there's a microwave available for reheating. Otherwise, these meals out will cost you big bucks over time. Add these costs to your list.
- **Transportation.** It might be extra gas money to get you back and forth every day. Or, it might be a public transportation pass or parking charges once you arrive at work. Add on any additional transport costs to your overall list of expenses.

If you've discovered that your income after additional costs barely exists, consider benefit packages including medical insurance and retirement plans and then discuss if it makes sense for both of you to work. This will obviously need to be a well thought out decision, but having the facts at hand might make it an easier decision overall. Cold hard numbers can take the emotional impact off almost any major decision a family needs to make. You might also find you can get just as much financial benefit from working only part-time (less childcare needs and fewer lunches out), if your family really needs the secondary income.

Savings Ideas for New Parents

That adorable little bundle of babyhood in your arms is enough to melt any heart, especially yours. Unfortunately, your finances may be melting just as fast at the additional strain of baby-related costs.

Here are a few savings tips from moms in the know. Keep in mind that frugality is more about what you don't buy, rather than what you do purchase—a frugal mind-set means getting by with less. Advertisers work overtime to get new parents (or grandparents) to spend on unnecessary stuff. What babies really need is unconditional love, warmth and comfort, food to fill their tummies, and some clothing and diapers.

- **Clothing.** Infants and toddlers grow out of clothes lightning fast! Plus their clothes go through some serious wear and tear with spills, stains and frequent laundering. So, be open to secondhand clothing—either at secondhand shops or by receiving hand-me-downs from friends and family. Secondhand is an especially nice option for special-occasion outfits that will be worn only once or twice. As soon as your child outgrows an outfit, do one of four things with it:
  1. Put it in storage for a younger sibling if you plan to have more children.
  2. Give it to a friend or family member for her child.
  3. Take it to a consignment shop for resale.
  4. Put it aside for a garage sale. If you plan to have a garage sale, try to have one every year. The clothes, toys, furniture and other baby accessories will still be in style, so you will get more money for them and they will sell faster.
- **Diapers.** Some parents swear by cloth diapers and insist that they're better for the environment and for the baby. And they can be easier on the pocketbook. But, be forewarned that they also mean a lot of additional work—extra laundry duty, for one. If you're going the route of disposable diapers, it's

more important than ever to learn to shop the sales. A great sale price (plus a money-saving coupon—which often can be found on a manufacturer's Web site) can easily save you 30–40 percent off the regular retail cost. Many moms also say that it's a newcomer's mistake to fall for the "pricier-the-diaper-the-better" mentality. Try some of the less expensive versions and save 40 percent right there and then. This is one product that might be far less to purchase when buying in bulk. Visit your local big box stores (such as Costco in the U.S.) and compare the price per diaper versus buying at the supermarket or drugstore.

- **Food.** If breastfeeding is a viable option for you, pursue it. It's the most natural way to feed your baby, and you'll save money on formula. Once your baby can begin eating solids, you can save money by making your own baby food. Homemade baby food is incredibly simple because babies just need good, pure puréed food to fill their little bellies. Puréed cooked veggies or fruit can be stored in ice cube trays and frozen for quick pop-out meals at a minute's notice. (Or whenever your baby's lungs make it known that he or she is hungry now.) Be sure to consult your baby's pediatrician for proper nutrition guidelines and instructions on what your baby's digestive tract can handle as the child continues to grow.

- **Necessities (and accessories).** A baby shower is a fantastic way for new parents to get the necessities and accessories they need to welcome their child home. Grandmothers-to-be, aunts-to-be and friends are often very eager to host a shower for the new mommy. If you are having a shower, be sure to register for gifts. The benefits of registering are three-

Baby Shower Savings

Here are some fun, low-cost ideas for throwing a fabulous, yet budget conscious baby shower.

1. Gifts. Choose gifts that are within your gift-giving budget and ones that are practical. The new mom will be more grateful for things she and her baby actually need, rather than just the cute fluffy stuff. Handmade gifts are also the most meaningful ones, so if you can paint, crochet, knit or sew, consider making your gift to save money while adding sentimental value.

2. Decorations. Skip paper banners and disposable decorations and plates and, instead, decorate with items that can be used in the baby's nursery. Gift trees and diaper pyramids assembled with ribbon look great and are practical. Use real tablecloths and your nice china to serve the food. It's a great excuse to actually use your nicest things and it makes an elegant impression.

3. Food matters. An impressive batch of cupcakes is very frugal to make. For about five to ten dollars, you can make dozens and decorate them as beautifully as in any gourmet bake shop with colorful clouds of icing and sprinkles. Get the guests to bring snacks, too—miniature munchies like cakes and sandwiches go perfectly with the baby theme.

fold: First your guests can select from gifts you truly want and need; second, it reduces the odds of receiving multiples of the same product; and third, many stores offer the registered parents a 10 percent discount on any unpurchased items left on the registry after the event.

JUNIOR SAVERS: TEACHING KIDS THE VALUE OF MONEY

This world is filled with all the wrong kinds of money consciousness for kids. They seem to think that money from Mom or Dad just appears out of thin air whenever it's needed—for the latest brand-name shoes, video game consoles, cell phones or laptops. This ain't the '50s anymore, sweetheart! (Or even the '90s, come to think of it.) Kids' dream purchases now are just as likely to cost hundreds of dollars as the twenty bucks it probably cost your parents to keep you satisfied.

Teaching kids to be financially responsible is not only important now—for your own sanity and budget—but also later on. Responsible kids and teens grow into adults who know their way around

The Real Value of a Buck

Count out one hundred pennies and then show your kids that ten dimes, twenty nickels or four quarters equals the same amount of money. (A quick trip to the bank for rolled coins will make this a lot easier.) Even though one dollar doesn't seem like a lot, teach kids that saving up those coins can quickly add up, so it's a great way to save for special items. An added lesson: Illustrate how much a dollar can buy in other parts of the world. Do the research and show how much one dollar can buy of basic essentials like wheat, rice, clean water or education in less fortunate areas of the world. For older kids, use this same approach when they want to buy a larger ticket item, such as a new gaming system. Show them in a visible way (perhaps in a chart) how much that expenditure would buy—comparing it to your monthly mortgage, utility bills, etc. Both methods will impress upon kids that every dollar has real value.

a bank statement. Kids who learn early on how to budget, save and shop carefully (not emotionally) will be less likely to incur huge amounts of debt and financial worries later. So, it's a true win-win situation with far reaching benefits for everyone.

Twelve Tips to Teach Money Skills to Kids

The following tips will help your children become financially aware early on in life. Maybe you're just learning some of these principles for the first time, too, never having had a parent who taught you money management skills. If so, you know better than anyone how much you wish you'd known this stuff earlier on, so don't hesitate to teach it to your kids! They need to know about money, especially in this money-mad world. Adjust and tweak the tips—like you do your budget—to come up with more ideas that will work well for your children's personalities and learning styles.

1. *You* **walk the walk.** Telling your kids to stay within their budget (their weekly allowance or part-time income) won't have a lot of merit if you don't do the same yourself. Make sure you walk the walk as far as money is concerned, and take your own finances as seriously as you expect them to. Be a role model they can look up to.

2. **Don't overwhelm them.** While helping your kids learn new money management skills, you don't need to bore them with long lectures. You'll have much greater success by approaching it more casually and naturally—talk to your kids at the grocery store while you're choosing your purchases. Ask them which product they think is the better bargain. Or, while shopping for clothes, get them to help you find a good deal for the money—not always the very cheapest item, but a

good quality garment for a fair price. Look through newspaper advertisements together before you go shopping so you know which stores have the best prices. Teach kids money lessons as they come up, not forcefully.

3. **Start early.** As soon as your children are old enough to understand the concept of paying money for things they'd like to own, give them small allowances of their own. Teach them from a very young age that they have to use their own money to get some of the things they want. Starting at about three or four years of age seems to work for most families, even if that allowance is only a dollar or two a week. An allowance teaches kids on many levels. They learn to save. They learn the value of a dollar. As the parent, you are responsible for setting the allowance. Use your budget to determine how much you can afford to pay in allowance per month. Then divide that figure evenly over the weeks and pay the allowance on a weekly basis. For young kids, even fifty cents a week will seem like a lot of money to them.

4. **Earning extra.** Kids shouldn't feel they're helping out around the house only to get paid. But, after the regular household chores are done, you can reward your kids for helping out with extra chores. Settle on a price with your child before he or she starts working. Fair's fair, after all.

5. **Teach them to save.** Savings are invaluable. Teach your kids early on to save a portion of their weekly allowance—from 10 to 20 percent or even more if they want to—into a piggy bank or into a savings account of their very own. They'll learn the joy of saving when they see the digits in the account grow and grow. Impress upon them that savings are just that,

money saved away for important future expenses, not a fund to be dipped into for impulse purchases. When your child gets his first job, help him open a checking account. Teach him how to balance a checkbook and be sure he does so on a regular basis.

6. **Anti-snobbery laws.** Teach your kids that cool stuff doesn't always have to come shiny and new in a plastic package from the store. Secondhand stuff is very cool, and kids who learn that early on also learn to stretch their dollars further. Teach kids that character and values are more important then appearances and possessions. Be sure they know their identity isn't shaped by what they own, but by what they do. You have to set the example here. If they see you valuing brand-names and expensive things, they will value them as well. If you are content with what you have, they will be, too.

7. **Back to school madness.** Reduce the cost of school supplies by carefully planning ahead. Large retailers lure customers with ultra bargains called loss leaders. Retailers are willing to lose money on these items, because they're pretty sure that once you're in the store you'll spend on other things. If you plan carefully and stock up on these necessities, and shop all the loss leaders at the different retailers, you'll supply your kids for less than you thought possible. And make sure to buy extras, otherwise come mid-term, you'll find yourself with a needy student and school supplies back up to premium prices. Also, make a list before you head out shopping, and tell your kids what essentials and extras you're willing to buy for them and which ones you'll expect them to contribute some of their allowance towards.

8. **Teach them about advertising.** Kids watch TV more than ever. Recent statistics show that the only activity they do more of is sleeping. Add to that the advertising strewn across the Internet, and you have a lot of advertisers aiming to get your kids' attention and their money. Teach your children that advertisers are paid to tempt people to buy stuff from cheeseburgers to video games, from candy to condos. Take time to teach them the difference between what's shown on the screen and what's real.

9. **Make them pay for it themselves.** Parents are obviously responsible for providing shelter, clothing and food for their offspring. But what about the pricey new gadget that everyone at school has and that your son is just begging for? If it's not an essential and it's out of your budget, then your kids will have to learn to save up and pay for it themselves. They'll also learn at the same time how much work goes into making a purchase over and above the necessities of life. Also, set budgets for the necessities and let the children supplement the budget if they insist on name brands and designer clothes. For example, if you plan to only spend twenty-five dollars on a pair of jeans, but your daughter wants a sixty-dollar pair, make her pay the additional thirty-five dollars. If your child doesn't have the extra money, she will have to wear the less expensive pair you buy or go without the jeans until she can save up for the more expensive pair.

10. **List pros and cons.** When your kids are eager to buy something special, teach them how to make a pros and cons list to help with their decision making. List all the reasons for and against this particular expenditure. Once they see in writing

how much money the need and how long they'll need to save in order to buy their dream item, it might suddenly seem less essential.

11. **Part-time jobs.** Younger kids can apply for their own paper route, a way that many successful business people began earning incomes of their own. Once in their mid to late teens, kids can look to fast-food joints or retail shops for part-time jobs to help supplement the allowance money you provide. It's great experience and teaches kids valuable lessons in responsibility.

12. **Charge rent.** No, your four year old doesn't have to pay rent. But, your children ages eighteen and over do! Set a reasonable amount that they can contribute towards that roof over their heads. This teaches them how to be financially independent and prepares them for when they move out on their own. If you don't want to take their money, you can put their rent money aside in a special account and return it to them when

Pack Their School Lunches

You can save a bundle on lunch fees by packing your children's lunches. Your kids will probably love this because they can pick the food they want to eat for lunch. Pack food that doesn't need to be refrigerated or reheated. Most schools also offer a free or reduced-price lunch program to families who meet specific income requirements. If you think you might qualify, ask for an application to the program at the school's office.

they move into a place of their own. They could use the money for furnishings or a down payment or a security deposit.

Now, let's be fair. When kids are taught the true value of money, it's very helpful, but kids are kids. (Even some of us grown-ups revert to childish ways now and again! Ahem …)

Kids need to have some fun along the way. Balance out all this new responsibility with fun activities that will show them that a frugal life isn't boring.

Twenty Low-Cost Activities for Kids

Here are some fun, low- or no-cost activities for kids, plus extra space for you to write down more ideas of your own, once you've been bitten by the inspiration bug. Delve into your own memory banks and retrieve the precious memories that matter most to you—time spent with family, getting to know your best friends, parties, vacations, etc. These activities will show your kids that having fun does not have to come with a substantial price tag.

1. **Lemonade stand.** This is an entrepreneurial adventure that can earn them a little extra income. Very handy for when they want to purchase something that you can't afford.

2. **Go fly a kite.** A wonderful activity for kids of all ages. You can purchase a basic kite for about ten bucks and it'll provide mornings and afternoons filled with fun. Or, you can construct your own kites with fishing line, small dowel rods, plastic trash bags and ribbons.

3. **Camping in the backyard.** Do you have no time or inclination to go out and camp in the great outdoors? (And possibly encounter bears? Yikes!) Instead, try that favorite family activity in your own backyard. Or, if the weather isn't cooperating,

take your good intentions indoors and set up a fort or tent where it's warm and cozy and safe. And, blessedly bug free.

4. **Garage sale or thrift shopping.** Now, here's some shopping that isn't so cash exhaustive. Teach kids that shopping can be fun when they have earned money to spend and when there's a legitimate need for a certain item. Your daughter needs some new (or new to her) jeans? Take her shopping and give her a challenge to get the nicest ones she can find at the thrift shop for what your budget allows. Shop garage sales to find unique items to decorate your kids' rooms.

5. **Fun in the kitchen.** Kids love to get creative in the kitchen. If they're really little and the idea of letting them loose in the kitchen fills you with dread, provide a foundation for them to have fun with—let them decorate cupcakes or oversized cookies that you've already baked. Kids also love making candies (pouring chocolate into molds is great fun when you peel away the mold to reveal the intricate design left behind) or making homemade bread and buns.

6. **Treasure hunts.** A particular favorite of my childhood, this is a kids' dream come true! Create a treasure map where each location holds a clue to the next location, and the end of the course has a hidden treasure.

7. **Make pizza.** This is a dual-purpose task. Not only does it keep your child entertained, but it also provides a meal for the family. Try a dessert pizza: regular pizza dough topped with sweet stuff instead of savory. Caramel or chocolate sauce or pie filling constitutes the sweet pizza sauce and add dessert toppings like coconut flakes, candies, chocolate shreds, dried fruit, nuts and marshmallows.

8. **Emerging photographer.** Digital cameras can be relatively inexpensive, making one worthwhile even for the junior frugalites in your home. If they show any interest in photography, a camera might make an ideal gift for them. There are sturdier cameras available now for little kids, able to withstand the rough and tumble treatment kids put it through. Encourage their creativity by going on photography jaunts, and then frame their best photos. An even less expensive option is to let the kids use your camera if they're old enough to be responsible with it.

9. **Pretty in paint.** Painting can bring out the creative genius in your child. And painting isn't only for budding artistes. Paint furniture and décor items to help your kids transform their room into a showpiece of their own personal style.

10. **Find natural treasures.** Challenge your kids to find an amazing treasure outdoors. It could be an especially beautiful leaf or a tiny ladybug. These finds can be the basis of a research project—search online or at the library to find out what kind of leaf it is they found or how ladybugs help us control pests.

11. **Find a treasure indoors.** Kids love to see old pictures of their parents, relatives and friends, especially those funny ones that were taken before the kids were born. Or, find an old memory in the house, tucked away in the unlikely form of a piece of furniture or an old sweater. This is a fun challenge that can end up taking many forms and creates bonding time with your child.

12. **Make a gift for someone else.** Create a jar of homemade hot cocoa mix (there are loads of free recipes for this on the Internet) or whip up chocolate chip cookies for a neighbor or

friend. "Just because" gifts are often the most cherished, and your kids see what their generosity can accomplish—pure joy for someone else.

13. **Make an imagination box.** Let the kids help fill it with crafty items that inspire creativity and then pull it out when the kids are bored.

14. **Make it yourself.** Bubbles, clay, paints, papier-mâché projects, frozen treats. Crafty stuff doesn't need to be of the scrap-booking or knitting variety; instead it can entail making fun stuff instead of buying it. Homemade bubbles, for instance, are a combination of dishwashing liquid and water and a makeshift bubble blowing wand. Homemade clay (think Play-Doh) has been a frugal favorite for decades and is just as good as store bought. Plus, the kids get to make their own dough before they mold it into something spectacular—a two-for-one creative activity.

15. **Toilet paper gone wild.** What kind of "outfit" can your kids create with TP? And what kind of fun mess can they create while they're at it? A great rainy day activity that guarantees loads of giggles. And, at the price of just one toilet paper roll, it's budget friendly.

16. **Science experiments.** Discover cool scientific experiments online that use common household ingredients as the base and teach your kids some scientific facts for low cost.

17. **Green thumbs start young.** If you have any outdoor space, or a few pots out on the balcony, let your kids grow their own plants. Take seeds from store-bought produce and grow a plant from them. Plant citrus seeds or pineapple tops to create new plants. An especially fun and fast project is to chop

off the greens of green onions and then replant the bulb in soil. Within a few days you'll have brand-new baby onions sprouting. Kids will love the quick results that they can eat.

18. **Water, water everywhere.** Add a sprinkler or a hose-drenched length of plastic to slide on out in the backyard for instant entertainment. Don't go overboard, or you'll see the costly end results on your next water utility bill.

19. **Write a letter, poem or story.** Writing is one of the best ways to vent one's emotions, no matter what those emotions happen to be. Ask your kids to write you a story; help get them started with a fun theme or a character that you want them to develop.

20. **No-cost activity jar.** Brainstorm more ideas with your kids and write them down on pieces of colorful paper. Toss all of the ideas into an oversized jar and let the kids reach in and randomly choose what their activity will be.

Your ideas:

_____

_____

_____

_____

_____

_____

_____

MONEY-CONSCIOUS PET CARE

Pet owners know that their pets are an important part of the family. Their unconditional love and those adorable eyes staring up at us are enough to keep us forever devoted. But, pet care can be pricey, a fact that many pet owners have experienced. Here, then, are some useful ways to reduce the overall cost of taking care of the family's friend, while keeping them healthy at the same time.

Food

Good, healthy food for your pets keeps them nourished and energized from the inside out. So, the cheapest brand of pet food just won't do. Instead, aim to find quality food that is also reasonably priced. Ask your pet's vet for a suggestion and do some research of your own to come up with a good middle-ground selection.

How Sales and Coupons Can Equal Big Savings

That $19.99 bag of dog food on sale is $14.99. Already a decent savings of 25 percent, but add a four-dollars-off coupon that you've been holding onto and that original twenty dollar sack of food is nearly half the price at $10.99! Stockpile this to last until the next bargain rolls around. (This is also proof of how vital it is to get a number of good coupons when they're available. Don't be shy, grab a handful!) If there's a limit of coupons per customer, take a family member or friend with you and send them through a different checkout lane so you can use all the coupons you need.

Some pet lovers swear by making their own pet food. Even though that sounds rather labor-intensive, it's really not. Good pet food, especially for dogs, all boils down to good quality protein—meat! The ingredients for making dog food, then, are really quite simple, but you will need to understand what to put together and how. This way you also

Regularly check the pet food manufacturer's Web site for coupons.

get the benefit of knowing exactly what ingredients go into the food your pet is ingesting, a luxury most of us don't have when relying on commercial mixes. Ask your vet if he or she recommends home-made food because your pup has specific nutritional requirements to be met, and many commercial foods are specifically formulated to meet these. Your vet will also be able to recommend recipes if you choose to make your own food. If you find your own recipe, run it by your vet before you make it and feed it to your pet to ensure that none of the ingredients are harmful and that the recipe is nutritionally sound.

If you're not excited about experimenting with homemade pet food production, rely instead on coupons and sales. Coupons for dog and cat food are common, and if you use high-value coupons during good sales, you can easily come away with your pet's preferred food for up to 60 percent off the regular prices. Stock up when these opportunities occur, so that you're well supplied until another sale arrives. Regularly check the pet food manufacturer's Web site for coupons. (Even without the coupons, waiting for good sales is the time to stock the pantry with pet food.) This money-saving technique also applies to other pet care essentials, such as cat litter and doggy treats.

Do-It-Yourself Pet Toys

No matter how much I spend on toys for my two cats, it's inevitable that the true winner is the aluminum foil ball that I scrunch together. That or the good old-fashioned cat favorite of a ball of yarn pleases them more than any fancy toy. So, don't feel guilty if you don't spend a mint on entertaining gadgets for your pets, because it seems that they usually show us up by preferring the basics anyway.

Try entertaining your pet with these:

- **Cat toys:** Cat fishing pole. This toy is worth its weight in gold (or in the minds of my cats, worth its weight in catnip). It is a simple plastic pole with a length of elasticized string and a plastic ball with jingly bells inside attached at the end of the string. My cats went bonkers for this toy! You can easily make this toy yourself with a dowel rod, some elastic, yarn or string, and a firmly attached ball. Balls of aluminum foil and yarn are great fun for cats, as are newspapers and cardboard boxes.
- **Dog toys:** Purchase Frisbees at dollar stores or garage sales. Or find them for free at trade shows and vendor booths. Take a walk to your neighborhood tennis courts when they are empty and you can pick up any stray balls left behind for free. Tie an old blanket or towel in a knot and use it as a tug toy. Taking the frugal theme to an extreme, consider good old sticks to play fetch with. When you think of the times your dogs are the happiest, the toys are usually the old standbys, not the posh and polished versions.
- **Toys for birds:** I have it on good authority that birds go wacky for a nice, shiny mirror. Make sure the mirror is in good shape and safe, so that their pointy beaks won't be able to wreak havoc. Like any pet, birds have their own unique

preferences, and sometimes are just as happy with some cardboard cutouts tied onto a length of string.

Watch the joyful expressions on your pets' faces and you'll see that they don't mind at all that their toys were snagged on the cheap. They'll never know that they were so friendly to the budget anyway. To them, fun doesn't come with a high price tag.

Veterinarian's Bills and Pet Insurance

We've already discussed how beloved our pets are to us. They love us simply and unconditionally—even when we're sprawled out on the couch battling a nasty cold, or when we're just not in peak form (such as before that first cup of java in the morning). So, of course their health is of vital concern to us pet lovers, but unfortunately the health of our pets also can come at a high premium.

Pet insurance can either be viewed as extravagant or, if you'd be willing to pay any price to keep your pet healthy, vital. Pet insurance helps you to cover the high costs of medical procedures for your pet that occur due to illness or accidents. If your pet requires emergency veterinary care, the attached bill can quickly escalate into thousands of dollars. Pet insurance can cost under ten dollars a month (but can be upwards of forty dollars for older pets), so for pet owners, it might be a logical way of handling these unexpected emergencies. Keep in mind, however, that pet insurance usually doesn't cover routine visits to the vet.

Keep your pets healthy by feeding them nutritious food, giving them regular exercise and grooming them regularly. Also, keep up with their vaccines and medication for heartworm and fleas. Don't overfeed them or feed them people food; it may be hard to resist that begging face, but they will be much healthier if you do.

More Ways to Save Money on Your Pets

1. **Not necessarily a pet sitter.** A trusted neighbor, friend or family member will likely not mind looking in on your pet while you're away. You can return the favor for them in the future when they travel.

2. **Pass by trendy pet stores.** The adorable displays of toys and gourmet foods come with a hefty price tag. Shop for food, toys and accessories at big-box stores or discount stores to save big. If you love the look of glamorous accessories, make them yourself. You'd be amazed what you can create with a few rhinestones and fabric paint. Try your hand at sewing your own pet bed.

3. **Baking soda means no odor.** For years, I've sprinkled some in my cats' litter box every time I change their litter, and it helps greatly. It naturally helps to overcome odor issues, without a fake flowery scent trying to mask it. Also use baking soda to sprinkle on the carpets if you have a little eau de pet scent going on in your home. Sprinkle it on, let it sit for fifteen minutes and then vacuum the baking soda and smells away.) Baking soda is way cheaper than any specialty pet odor control product.

4. **Vinegar for flea control.** Even though it sounds unlikely, pouring a tablespoon of apple cider vinegar in your dog's water dish will help to naturally repel fleas. You can also combine one part apple cider vinegar to one part water and use as a natural flea repellent spray on your dog's fur.

5. **Dog and cat shampoo—baking soda!** Again, the good old box of white stuff comes in incredibly handy. Take a handful and scrub it through your pet's fur (which has already been wet

with water). Give them a scrub, and then rinse thoroughly. After they've dried, give them a good brushing for a gorgeous coat worthy of many medals. The baking soda will also help remove any lingering "wet dog" odors.

6. **Selecting a vet.** Obviously, you want a veterinarian who is compassionate and kind, but you'll also want to compare fees and costs because these can vary greatly. Ask your friends who they take their pets to for a good referral. If there's a veterinary university near your home, check into taking your pet there for excellent treatment.

7. **Prevent accidents before they happen.** Especially if you have kittens or puppies in the house, you'll want to look at the house as if a baby were crawling around. Common household products, cleaners or even innocent plants can cause your pet harm. Do your research and prevent an unnecessary vet visit and pain and suffering for your pet. Keep your cats indoors and keep your dogs on a leash or fenced in so they can't run into traffic.

8. **Get pet's meds online.** Routine medications like flea treatments and heartworm pills cost far less if you order them online. Remember that generic medications are the same as their costlier brand-name counterparts, so don't feel guilty about purchasing them.

9. **Groom at home.** Simple grooming tasks such as baths, brushing and clipping claws are easily performed at home. But be careful when you clip your pets' claws. If you mistakenly cut into the quick of the nails, it will cause them a lot of pain.

10. **That's a lotta litter.** Buy bulk boxes of low-dust cat litter for less at big-box stores. Instead of purchasing scented varieties

(which can aggravate and irritate your cats' lungs), sprinkle in some baking soda every time you change the litter.

Each member contributes a vital part to your family's dynamics and energy. Their assistance and enthusiasm for your new frugal lifestyle, will give you the encouragement you need to keep on track, too.

SPENDING CHALLENGE

1. **The family that spends (time) together saves together.** Make a list of fun activities that everyone in the family will enjoy that are either free or very low cost. Whoever comes up with the most imaginative ideas should win a no-cost prize such as getting to decide which movie the family will watch or receiving a "freedom pass" from chores for a day.

2. **Feed another family.** Saving allows you the freedom to help others. When there are good sales at the supermarket (especially when matched with a coupon), get a few items to take to the local food bank. It's an invaluable real-life lesson for children and adults alike. Your careful spending will give you a little extra cash that you can use to benefit other people beyond your family.

3. **One month of reduced pet spending.** For one month, cut back on non-essential pets' expenses. (Nothing vital like vet visits, please; we want our furry friends kept healthy.) Some ways you can chop spending include grooming your pet yourself or making homemade treats instead of the gourmet ones you usually buy. Keep track of how much you saved.

5 | Living Large at Home for Less

Home sweet home is the ultimate dream, but finding an ideal home that fits your family's needs and your budget can seem like a dream that will never be a reality. Home ownership equalling happiness is a concept that has been deeply ingrained in us. For some, that dream home might be a high-rise condo located downtown amidst towering skyscrapers. For others, it's a rambling country home in the greenery of nature. No matter what kind of house means home to you, housing is generally the largest outgoing expense of any budget. Your original idea of a dream home might have to be modified dramatically to make it fit with your financial reality. In the meantime, you might end up finding happiness in the least expected places.

Besides paying for the physical dwelling itself, we also need to evaluate where money is spent on making your home run—from utilities to furnishings. All of these expenses can add up quickly and just as rapidly drain our budgets. In this chapter, you'll discover ways to create a comfortable home, minus the extravagant price tags.

FINDING AFFORDABLE HOUSING

It may be the ultimate dream for many folks to own their very own home, but owning is a decision that must be made logically, not emotionally. As we have seen all too clearly over the past years, owning a home is not the best choice for everyone. Simply stated, if you can't afford to own a home—with all the additional costs associated with home ownership—then renting is your best option.

Questions to Ask Before Deciding to Rent or Own

There is an argument for and against renting. Many people would have you believe that renting is the ultimate way to waste your money, that, in essence, you're throwing away money each and every month and thousands of dollars every year. But it all depends on your personal circumstances. With that in mind, here are some things to consider before making this huge decision.

Owning a home is not the best choice for everyone.

1. How long do you plan to stay in the home? Purchasing a home comes complete with plenty of additional costs, such as closing costs, Realtor commission and other legal fees. So it only makes sense to purchase a home if you plan to stay there for a number of years, ideally at least five. The longer you own the home, the more time you have to build equity. If you sell the house after only a few years, you may end up selling the house for less than you paid for it, depending on the housing market. As with the stock market, the longer you're in the housing market, the less you'll be affected by any sudden ups and downs in prices.

2. Do you want (or can you handle) the responsibility that

comes with owning? On the surface, buying makes all the sense in the world because, after a certain number of years of paying the mortgage, you can rightfully say that you own the property. But, do you have the income needed to pay for all the maintenance costs of the property? As a renter, those costs are included in your rent and the landlord is responsible to do repairs and replace broken appliances. As an owner, it all lands firmly at your feet.

3. Do you look at your home as an investment? Over time, as rental costs can increase, your mortgage will stay relatively the same, depending on interest rates. The cost paid in rent isn't recoverable, as it is with a mortgage. Over the long term, housing is usually a safe investment, but as we've seen recently, that isn't always true. Are you committed to living in the house for an extended period of time, or are you planning to live there for just a few years before moving on to other pastures? If you're not settled on an area (or in life), maybe this isn't the time for you to buy.

4. Can you afford a mortgage? For many, the dream of owning their own home is so instilled in them, that they make major emotional decisions that can turn into a financial maelstrom. Make a detailed budget of all your expenses, using your current rental rate, and then compare it with what your home ownership costs will be. Keep in mind all the additional utilities, taxes, insurance and repairs that are part of owning a home. See if you can make the budget work and successfully make ends meet each month. If not, then you're not ready to take on a home until you can earn more money or cut back on other expenses.

Mortgages

If you've decided that buying is indeed the right option for you, get ready to do some exhaustive research. Every bit of time spent researching different lenders and interest rates will pay off hugely. Why? Consider that with a typical mortgage, you can end up paying two times the value of your home by the time you sign the last mortgage check after twenty-five years! With that in mind, try to keep the length of your mortgage term to no more than twenty years, max. This applies to North America and the UK, where it's become more and more common to see forty-year mortgage terms. In Scotland, the length of term can go even longer, with the Bank of Scotland offering a maximum mortgage term of fifty-two years! Regardless of where you live, make it your goal to have the shortest mortgage term

Dig Deep for a Down Payment

The more money you have saved as a down payment before you purchase your home, the better. Ten percent should be the minimum you aim to save, and the minimum amount that many financial institutions now require. Heading into a financial institution with a large amount of money already accumulated gives you a better shot at a lower interest rate, plus it will lower your monthly mortgage payment, which will make life easier for you every month when you sign the check. Yes, it means waiting a little longer before purchasing your first home, but patience is, after all, a very valuable virtue. It helps you to keep a logical outlook on home buying, not an emotional one.

you can possibly afford; in the long run, you'll easily save tens of thousands of dollars in interest charges.

Before ever attempting to get a mortgage, you need a long-term plan of attack in order to get one that is in your best interest—that of course, means one with the lowest interest rate. The less credit card debt you have, the better it looks to potential lenders. When you apply for a mortgage, the bank will consider the savings you've managed to accumulate for a down payment. They'll also look at your other debt, including credit card debt and loans. Make your financial portfolio look good by working to lower your debts before you apply for a mortgage. It's a good idea to pull your own credit report before you apply for a mortgage. You'll be able to see what your lenders will see and can work to resolve any issues that may hurt your chances of getting a mortgage or issues that may keep you from getting a lower interest rate.

Research mortgages ahead of time, and talk to lots of different lenders so you know what the best possible interest rate is and make it your goal to get that rate, or as close to it as possible. Every seemingly tiny drop in interest, even if it's only a tenth of a point, will save you thousands of dollars over the life of the loan. See if your preferred lender will negotiate to match a competitor's rate. They sometimes will, especially if your credit is good and you seem like a worthy client.

After you sign the mortgage, right from the first month, make it a goal to make consistent extra payments on your mortgage. (To do so, make sure at the time of signing that you're entitled to do this without extra fees.) Even if it's only twenty extra bucks, if it's consistent, it'll peel off thousands of dollars in interest charges from your loan over its lifetime. Large payments are great—when you

Assumable Mortgages

Another option when buying a house is an assumable mortgage. This is an arrangement where a buyer takes over the seller's outstanding mortgage on a property. Usually this is a good option only if you can't get a traditional mortgage or if the pre-existing mortgage has a lower interest rate than what is currently available. The buyer pays the difference between the balance of the mortgage and the value of the house as a down payment. So, if a house is worth $150,000, but the seller's assumable mortgage is only $120,000, the buyer has to put $30,000 as a down payment. Never assume a mortgage that is higher than the value of the property. When researching an assumable mortgage, a good place to start is at the United States Department of Housing and Urban Development (HUD) government Web site: hud.gov, which provides a wealth of information on all types of mortgages.

receive large amounts of money unexpectedly, such as a bonus or rebate—but the real issue here is consistency. The banks make more money the longer you have a mortgage outstanding, so take back that money by paying extra whenever possible. Paying bi-weekly instead of just once a month will also take a couple of years off the life of your loan.

Renting a House

If, on the other hand, your choice is to rent a single-family house, there are still many considerations to take into account to save cash. For the most part, this requires a bit of negotiating on your lease.

You can negotiate for lower rent, and/or rental perks. And, of course, the greater freedom that comes with renting means that if you don't like the terms where you're at, you can always pick up and move once your lease has ended.

Sometimes, a landlord is willing to negotiate lower rent, especially if he or she is the property owner, as opposed to an employee at a large property management firm. Ask if the rent is negotiable, or if you could help with yard work or property upkeep, etc., to receive a discount on rent. It may be worth your while to help out around the property if it means your rent is lower.

Apartments Are Homes, Too

Apartments might not be the dwelling you envision in your dreams, but the reality is that apartments make ideal homes for millions of people around the world. Apartments come in all shapes and sizes. Most people think of large complexes or towering apartment buildings, but in many areas, larger, older homes have been converted into apartments. There are also duplexes and fourplexes that are smaller buildings and feel more like a single-family home. With a little love and decoration, an apartment home can become as warm and inviting as any single-family dwelling. Plus, if your budget is small, they also provide you with a home of your own minus many of the expensive costs associated with owning a house—things like taxes, repairs, insurance and additional utilities that are often included in rent.

SAVE ON UTILITIES AND BIG TICKET ITEMS

Once you've got a home that comfortably fits your budget and lifestyle, you need to juice it up! You need to learn how to save on making your home run—all of the utilities that provide heat and light to your home, plus the larger items that fill it up and make it livable and lovable.

Save on Electricity

- **Remember light switches.** Turn them off when you're not in the room! Ask at a hardware store about "task lighting" solutions. These motion-detecting devices will turn the lights on when you need it and, after a certain period of time, will turn the lights back off again if there is no movement in the room. If you have forgetful family members who leave lights on, this might be a painless way to save. They're also a good security feature.

- **Don't overcharge.** Whether it's your laptop or cell phone, once it's charged up, unplug it. Otherwise it continues to use up electricity without adding any extra life to your favorite gadget. And don't forget to unplug the charger from the wall. Plugged-in chargers continue to draw energy regardless of whether a device is attached to them or not. This is a huge waste of energy.

- **Power strips.** With one flick of a switch, energy-sucking computers, printers, fax machines and more can be turned off of the power grid. Use power strips for your entertainment center, too. Any device that uses a remote control draws extra energy even when it is turned off because the device is in standby mode for the remote. Turn off the power strips when you go to bed, and when you go away on vacation. Why pay for powering machines you're not even using?

- **Fan power.** Keeping cool during the summer feels like a full-time job. Keep the heat out by closing blinds and curtains during the hottest part of the day (late morning to late afternoon) and utilizing rotating fans, and you'll keep your home cooler for less money than it costs to run an air conditioner.

- **Let the sun shine in, sometimes.** In the summer, there's so much sun around here that I hardly have to turn a light on. In the evening, open the curtains to let sunlight in. The sun will be lower in the sky so it won't be as hot, and you'll be able to keep your lights off until late in the evening.

- **AC action plan.** Air conditioners are energy drains, but if you need to run one, choose an energy-efficient model. Keep heat-producing devices such as lamps or computers away from the AC. Cool only the rooms you are in regularly. On smaller models, use a timer setting and only use it as often as is necessary. Don't run it constantly. Set the temperature to a medium coolness, because the coldest setting won't cool the room any faster, but it does work the machine harder.

- **Line up that laundry.** In warmer months, dry clothes out on a line. You save money, and get to feel like a homier, earthier kind of person. Lines can be found for purchase at any hardware store, and clothespins are a few dollars for dozens. In winter, use drying racks indoors.

- **Hair *au naturel* helps.** Cut back on hair drying and styling in the summer. Let your natural hair style do its thing, getting as curly or wavy as it wants to. You'll save a little money (and keep the temperature down in your home), and your hair will get healthier at the same time! Plus the humidity will likely undo all of your work anyway.

- **Make an appliance list.** Make a complete list of all of the appliances in your home. Become aware when electricity is being used and make it a goal to reduce the energy consumption on half the items at first, and eventually on as many devices as possible. Awareness here is the key.

- **Dishwasher.** Run it only when it's full and run it at night when electricity rates are generally lower. (To find out specifically when the lowest rates are in your area, call your electric company.) Save even more energy by turning off the heat-drying mode and let the dishes air dry in the dishwasher. Don't rely entirely on the dishwasher. Sometimes it's faster, easier and more frugal to wash a few dishes by hand.

- **Refrigerator and freezer.** Open the doors as little as possible. Know exactly what you want to get before you open the door and then shut the door as soon as you can. Don't stand there staring inside for five minutes. Every time you open the door to your refrigerator or freezer, the internal temperature rises, making them work harder. The longer the doors are open, the warmer they get. Plus the temperature changes are not good for food safety.

- **Microwave mania.** To slash electricity usage, run this appliance more and run the oven less, especially in the summer when it also cuts down on heat accumulation.

- **No-go door zone.** Don't be tempted to keep opening the oven door to sneak a peek at dinner. It lowers the temperature inside and makes your oven work harder. Look through the window instead, since that's its purpose in the first place. And, shut the power off about five minutes before your recipe is done; the oven will stay hot and the dish will continue cooking, but you will save energy.

- **Get liddy with it.** Add a lid on top of that pot and the water will boil much quicker. Your chemistry teacher would've explained it in terms of kinetic energy, but I'll explain it by saying that it'll reduce the time it takes your food to cook and will, therefore, lower your bills.

Save on Water Bills

- **Showers vs. baths.** A quick shower uses less water compared to a full-tub bath. (Remember, that means a five minute shower.) Test yourself to see if showering really does save water by plugging the tub and see how much water accumulates during your average shower. If the tub is more than halfway full when you are done, consider taking shorter showers or take a bath in a quarter-full tub.
- **Install water-saving showerheads.** It can reduce the amount of water flow by up to 60 percent!
- **Don't be a drip.** It's staggering that just one consistently dripping faucet can waste up to fifty gallons of water in one week! Take on the simple fix-it task yourself by getting out the pliers and tightening the nut or washer on the faucet.
- **Water the grass.** That's right, the grass. Not the side of the house, the edge of your car and the sidewalk! Adjust those sprinklers to accurately target the flowers and grass that actually need a drink. If you water early in the morning or late in the evening, your grass and flowers will be able to utilize their healthy beverage before the sun dries things out.
- **Bottle your own water.** Keep a reusable bottle on hand for your drinking water every day, and continue to refill it all day, then pop it into the dishwasher at night. There will be

far fewer glasses to wash at the end of the day. Each family member should have his or her own bottle.

- **Brush and floss with no water loss.** Brush your teeth with the tap turned off, and then turn it on right at the end to rinse your mouth and your toothbrush.
- **Lower the flow on toilets.** Toilet flushes account for 40 percent

Appliances

Replacing antiquated appliances sometimes saves you money over the long run because they run much more efficiently. The guiltiest energy consuming appliances are ones that either add heating or cooling to your home, such as your furnace, air conditioner, refrigerator or clothes dryer. Keep in mind the original price you pay for a new appliance, plus something called a "second price," that is, the cost of the energy needed to run the machine. Take both into account when purchasing a new appliance. This is made easy for you by clearly marked energy consumption labels on all new appliances.

Don't dream big when purchasing a shiny new appliance. No doubt a monolithic fridge looks impressive in the well-lit showroom, but the cost of running that beast—the second price—might not impress you nearly as much. Choose the size of appliance you and your family actually need. Besides, we're not the types to be impressed by ostentatious appliances, now are we? I thought not.

Do some research before going to the stores so that you won't make a decision based entirely on how the device looks, but rather on how it will perform over time. Also check out consumer reviews online, a fantastic way to see what owners are saying about that exact appliance.

of your home's water usage. If your toilet was made before 1992, it could use up to seven gallons of water per flush! Consider replacing the toilet with a more water-efficient model. If that's not in the budget, there are kits out there that can help you improve your toilet's efficiency. The best part is you don't have to be a plumber to install them. Find them at your local hardware store.

Save on Heating Costs

- **Fireplaces.** If you have a fireplace or wood-burning stove, you can reduce your reliance on the furnace by feeling the burn! Get firewood for free by simply keeping your eyes open—watch when people are cutting down old trees. We have one friend who is famous around our neighborhood for this technique, and he always has plenty of good wood to burn over the winter. Often, people don't want the bother of paying anyone to haul away the unwanted wood and they are more than happy to give it away.

- **Insulation.** Insulation basically wraps up your entire home and protects it from the elements in a way similar to how a warm sweater keeps you cozy in winter. If you live in a newer home, the likelihood is that the insulation is more modern and efficient. In older homes, however, check to make sure that some heat-sucking areas, such as the attic, are insulated.

- **Prevent leaks.** Installing weather stripping around doors and windows throughout your house means that your home is sealed tighter, and heat won't leak out. Specially designed plastic cling wrap for windows also prevents leakage and is very easy to install. All are available at hardware stores. Thick curtains will also help cut out drafts around windows and keep heat from escaping through the glass. A rolled up towel or blanket also can shut out drafts under doors.

- **Close registers.** Close off the heat registers in rooms you rarely use and keep the doors to those rooms closed. Why heat a room no one uses?
- **Control the temperature.** Turn down your thermostat at night and during the day when you are out of the house. Extra blankets should keep you cozy in bed. Use electric blankets if you get really cold; an even cheaper option is a hot-water bottle.

Save on Telephone and Internet

Gone are the days when talking to your beloved over the phone ended up costing you hundreds of dollars a month. (Ahh … I personally remember those days with a pang!) Now, basic plans usually include plenty of long-distance minutes per month, or unlimited plans let you jabber away to your heart's content for one basic price. To save even more, get rid of any features you really don't need. See if your phone/cable provider offers a bundle package that combines your phone, Internet and cable TV bills into one lowered rate.

Do You Need Both?

Do you need both a landline phone and a cell? Decide which one you use the most, and which one you can get for the cheapest amount, and stick with one or the other. More and more people are getting by just fine these days with a cell alone.

Cell phones have taken over the inflated pricing of old-fashioned long-distance charges. Save on cells by not signing on to long-term contracts and by researching to compare all of the different plans available to you. Determine what you need the phone for and how many minutes you'll realistically use before you ever go looking at phones. And, by using pay-as-you-go cards, you can keep cell bills down. Once the minutes on the card are eaten up, you simply can't use the phone until you go get the card refilled. It's a great budget-stretching tip.

If you don't really need the Internet at home, just use an Internet café occasionally to check e-mails or visit favorite Web sites. For a buck or two, you can browse the Net for about an hour. Or, get Wi-Fi access for free on your laptop at local coffee shops, libraries, restaurants and even airports if you happen to be travelling. We don't all need the Internet at our fingertips every moment of the day. People got by without it quite successfully for, let's see, thousands of years!

Save on Entertainment

When cutting back on unnecessary expenses, you might decide to get rid of expensive cable packages altogether. With TV on demand available on the Internet (most shows are posted on the network's Web site the day after their original air date and are available for a few weeks) to Netflix offering unlimited movies and TV shows on their new Netflix player at no extra cost, it seems that the days of pricey cable may be numbered.

FURNITURE AND DÉCOR: FASHIONABLE AND FRUGAL

Imagine a home that you love visiting because it's so incredibly comfortable. It might not look like a pristine show suite from a newly built home, but the cozy sofas just beckon you to curl up on them with a cup of tea and a good book. The kitchen is the hub of activity, filled with conversation and goodies. It's not the house itself that makes the space such a retreat; it's more of the personality of the people within it that's expressed through furnishings and decorations.

This is where you get to turn your house into a real home—a lived in, comfortable space where people want to gather. These little items aren't exactly essential, but do allow you to express your personality through those walls that surround you. Decorating the *Living Large on Less* way means making your home an expression of yourself at a price you can afford, and it means having fun in all sorts of creative ways.

> It's not the house itself that makes the space a retreat; it's the personality expressed through the décor.

Finding Furniture ... For Less

You might think that good quality furniture is beyond your monetary reach but, thankfully, that isn't the case. When it comes to buying lovely furniture for bargain basement prices, the attribute you really need is patience. So, if your kids need a bed tonight, you'll likely have to go get one your budget allows at a discount store. But, for those pieces that you'd like to add to your home, but which aren't absolutely necessary, wait a little while and enjoy the hunt. Such patience can net you some amazing finds.

My favorite way of finding gorgeous furniture on the cheap is online, at local classified sites such as Craigslist and Kijiji. People who are redecorating their homes, or perhaps in the middle of a cross-country move, just want their stuff gone and gone now to make room for their new furniture or new lives. This means great bargains are to be had because these same people are often willing to slash prices. The same holds true of garage sales or moving sales, so it pays to check these out, as well. And never be shy to offer a lower price! Pieces with good bones can be repainted, refinished or refurbished to breathe new life into them. Call it furniture CPR.

Other Ways of Finding Cheap-o Furniture

- **Curbside furniture store.** In the small town where most of my extended family lives, they have a yearly spring clean where people pile up unneeded items on the curb. Among those are beautiful pieces of furniture! People can literally go help themselves before the town trucks come along to take the stuff away. If your town has a spring clean, too, take advantage of it. But let the upholstered stuff go, because you never know what little critters or mold issues might be lingering there.
- **Let family and friends know.** Let everyone know what items you're looking for. They might not have anything, but they might know someone at work or in the neighborhood who does. Letting everyone know that you're looking for furniture will get the ball rolling.
- **Furniture swap.** Swap the stuff you don't need with friends for the stuff you do need. It helps everyone equally. You can accomplish this by sending out an e-mail to a few friends with a list of the stuff you have to swap and a wish list of your own.
- **Check posted signs at apartment/condo complexes.** Not everyone who's moving bothers to post an ad in the paper or

Get Your Leafy Greens: Houseplants

A house seems friendlier and cosier once a few houseplants get tossed into the mix. They even work as beautiful air filters to naturally purify the air in your home. Ask friends if they have cuttings of their houseplants to share, or, for a buck or two, get baby plants from the nursery. Once they're healthy and thriving, you can take cuttings of them and create more and more plants from that original growth. I love planting seeds from citrus fruits or replanting the bulbs of green onions to create new plants direct from the produce department. You can buy unusual seeds, such as coffee seeds, and have a plant that also works as an interesting conversation piece.

online, but they might put up a sign saying what stuff they need to purge before moving. As moving day approaches, they're more likely to want the stuff off their hands—and you can get it for cheap. Be confident with those negotiating skills.

- **Yard sales.** Like many frugal-finding techniques, these can be real hits or misses. Train yourself to look for the quality stuff that will last, not junk.

- **Thrift shops and secondhand stores.** Look for pieces with great lines that will look incredible once you've stylized them. Chairs can look entirely different once you repaint them or update the fabric. Almost anything outdated can be freshened up to feel more relevant.

- **Newspapers and community papers.** Check out the classifieds for listings of the best auctions, moving sales or yard sales to visit. They also have a separate section for used furniture for sale. Check your local paper's Web site to see if the classified ads are posted online.

Fourteen Ways to Stylize Your Home for Less

1. **Ask a friend.** Whatever you need, well, just ask for it! Ask handy friends with a tool bench how much it would cost to build a bookshelf or two. Barter instead of paying—maybe you could clean their house or paint a room in exchange for their labor. And then all you need to pay for are the materials. Friends and family can also assist you with decorating chores such as painting for the cost of some pizza and beers.

2. **Color it wonderful.** Don't be afraid of adding bright splashes of color to your space. A home filled entirely with neutral shades seems unbearably blah. Color cheers us up. The same holds true for flashy patterns—while too much would be overwhelming, a bit adds flair. Be selective with where you paint. Painting one accent wall will take less paint than painting the entire room. It also lets you use an intense color without overwhelming the space.

3. **Decorate as you'd dress.** If you love wearing the colors, then it's logical that you'll like having those same colors around you in your home. Love flashy colors? Prefer classic patterns? Then you'll likely enjoy the same style and patterns in your space. Take a look through your closet and dresser to get inspired to decorate.

4. **Get inspired by designers.** But only find *inspiration* this way! If you search through expensive online stores and end up at the checkout, your budget will never forgive you. Instead, check

out the trendiest online shops and see what designers are offering this season. Then make it your goal to match their coolness factor with your own handiwork.

5. **Sew it beautiful.** Find inspiration for easy-sew decorating projects at the library. It's *très chic* to make it yourself, or get a talented friend (or Mom!) to help you out. (If you're like me and can't sew a straight seam to save your life, look for books filled with no-sew fabric decorating ideas—using glue guns or staples instead of needle and thread.)

6. **Can't beat the sheet.** As already admitted, I'm no seamstress, so when it came to covering a boring wall in our living room, I used two twin sheets in my favorite shade of green to add texture and interest. The result? A cool wall, minus the paint. I stuck the sheets to the wall using small brass tacks. I'll plaster over the small holes before we move. Sheets can also be useful for covering an ugly sofa or tying over a chair.

7. **Minus the installation.** I love IKEA stuff because it's reasonably priced and fun. But, neither my husband nor I are geniuses with hand tools, so our IKEA creations never look the same as they did on display. Save the hassle by checking out secondhand stuff online at Craigslist. Someone else already put it together so you don't have to, and you'll pay about half the price.

8. **Check out the discount stores.** Just like you can't be a snob when shopping for clothes, you can't discount the discounters for décor, either. Bargain stores have serious design finds these days. Check out the clearance shelves for ridiculous savings and find a fashionable piece for your home space for less.

9. **Go lower still—dollar stores.** Keep an open mind and browse through a dollar store. Besides some really tacky stuff (which there undoubtedly is), you can search to find treasures. I've found gorgeous, name-brand candles and a beautiful painting for the bathroom (that went so perfectly I couldn't believe I'd snagged art for a buck! Less than buying the paint would've cost me!). Keep an open mind, but also don't get bogged down with a bunch of junk you don't need.

10. **Auctions (both online and offline).** Local auction houses hold lot sales where you can purchase housewares and furniture for great prices. Online auction sites like eBay have everything you can ever imagine needing for your home.

11. **Pick an element, any element.** A bright, bold piece of art. A comforter with an array of colors. An outrageous rug. Whatever it is, pick your favorite piece and then design the room and color scheme around it.

12. **Yes, that's my headboard.** A rectangular canvas covered with your favorite art can replace a traditional headboard. An old, painted door can do the same or even a length of fencing from the hardware store. (Ideal for a garden or cottage-inspired space! Paint it your favorite color, or paint it white and add hand-painted tendrils of greenery and blooms.)

13. **Smart art.** If you're at all artistically inclined, you can fill your walls with your own works. Figure out the colors first, and then set your imagination free. You can view art online to get inspiration. Even blocks of contrasting color set against a vibrant shade can turn your wall from blah to noticeable.

14. **Hardware store housewares.** Copper piping, chain-link fence, wooden fencing, bricks … all inspired ideas for décor

projects! Piping can be attached to the walls and then use hooks to store kitchen utensils, office supplies or crafting supplies. Search the stores to find cheap supplies you can re-envision to meet your needs.

Pretty in Paint: Ten Ways to Rejuvenate

Paint is a fairly inexpensive way to re-envision a room, a piece of furniture or a wall. But, you can save even more by asking at the paint store what they do with cans of incorrectly mixed paint. Some stores also have a policy to purchase back cans of unused paint from customers, so ask a sales associate where those cans are stored and see if one is the right shade for you. If you know of friends or neighbors who have recently painted their home or interior, ask if they have any extra paint they'd like to get rid of. They'll be glad to pass on the pesky leftovers, and you can snag some lovely new paint for free. Win-win!

1. **Stain it.** Beautiful natural wood doesn't need coatings of paint. Make real wood even lovelier by staining it a complementary shade, and let its goodness shine through.

2. **Stencil it.** Stencils can be Victorian in nature, or totally modern. Just imagine a cute dresser painted turquoise and emblazoned with big white polka dots for your daughter and you can see that stencils can be very fresh indeed.

3. **Mirror makeover.** Find a mirror at a thrift shop that has an interesting shape. Spray paint the frame in the color of your choice, and then finish with a coat of spray sealer. It'll look like a boutique item and only cost you around ten dollars to create it. The latest trend is to remove the mirror and replace it with bold printed wallpaper or fabric to make wall décor

that is truly one of a kind. Or, for a girls' room, it would make an ideal "frame" for her favorite pictures.

4. **Door power.** I just love an old door, rich with nicks and damage that scream character. Instead of replacing a great old door, repaint it instead, and replace the doorknob if you'd like to make the whole thing look newer.

5. **Floors.** I can almost see you rolling your eyes from here, but in certain cases, paint really is the best way to add life and color to your floors. If you have cheap, old wooden floors that are really beat up or cement floors in your basement, get a can of paint. Purchase a heavy-duty variety that will stand up to traffic and then a few coats of sealant over the top. Remember that it will take a couple of days for the paint and sealer to completely dry, so feet off!

6. **Walls have it.** Of course, the first thing most of us envision when we head to the paint store is revitalizing our walls. And no wonder—a fresh coat of paint is the easiest, fastest and cheapest way to change the vibe of a room. Paint an accent wall in one striking color to add serious dimension and interest. Or, paint a deeper complementary tone on the bottom, split the wall with a simple chair rail, and paint a lighter tone on top.

7. **Splattery art.** Pick some colors that match or contrast the rest of the room, get a big canvas, and get messy. Bold art is only a few splatters away with your paint brush. No true artistic talent is required.

8. **Try a technique.** Use special techniques to add texture and interest to boring walls. Rag rolling involves dipping crumpled rags in thinned paint (about one part water to two parts

paint) and then rolling the rag across an already painted wall. Practice before you try on the wall to make sure you have the technique down. Home makeover shows and Web sites offer great inspiration and instruction for these techniques.

9. **Paint kitchen cabinets.** If your can't afford to replace old cabinets, painting them can add a whole new, fresh dimension to your kitchen. Be sure to choose a scrubbable surface paint so that inevitable splatters can be cleaned up with ease.

10. **My, what a mural.** Think only real artists can create a mural? Think again! If you have some basic artistic talents, you might surprise yourself with what glories you can create on the walls in your home. Check out some books from the library that inspire you, particularly some on mural or large-scale decorative painting. The how-to books will give you great ideas and techniques, like using an overhead projector to help you get your design on the wall. Even books of classical paintings can awaken your inner artiste. For kids' rooms, a bright mural can change the whole personality of a room.

Five Ways With Wallpaper

Wallpaper has come an awfully long way since your Aunt Peggy's nasty florals that appeared to be attacking the walls. Ask at the paint store for free wallpaper samples and you can do some of the following crafts for no cost. Keep in mind that some wallpaper can be very expensive, so stock up at discount stores rather than specialty stores, or else shop the sales or purchase quantities online.

1. **Art's my name.** Wallpaper can be so striking that it serves as art all on its own. All you need is a big frame to showcase it and you have fresh art for a few bucks. Or, take tiny square

samples of wallpaper and make a wallpaper mosaic to frame and hang. You can do the same thing with paint color cards.

2. **Think on the box.** Wallpaper covered boxes not only look coordinated (especially if you pile a few staggered sizes together), but they hold junk for cheap. Great for office or craft-supply storage. Coordinate other office essentials (such as straight-sided trash cans) by covering them with the same wallpaper.

3. **Accents on furniture.** Old furniture looking bland? Freshen it up with elements from your favorite wallpaper. Simply sand down the surface first, and then apply. This is best done as detail work, like drawer fronts or the top of a dresser, not over the entire piece, which can look overdone.

4. **Tray.** An old tray can make a perfect gift by enlivening it with some pretty wallpaper. Wallpaper samples can be useful here—create a pretty mosaic of wallpaper across the top of the tray using bits and pieces of different patterns. Then seal with a few coats of varnish and allow plenty of time to dry.

5. **Wall cutouts.** Cut out major components of the wallpaper and then create a design on the wall. It's a fun and easy way to give a wall new life and a fashionable state of mind. Those cutouts are also useful for decorating boring office storage units, bookshelves and kids' furniture.

Don't let these ideas limit you, but let them rev up your brainstorming. If you see a surface in your home that needs a little face-lift, see if wallpaper might do the trick.

CLEANING ON THE CHEAP

It takes only three words to sum up healthy housecleaning for less. *Baking soda* and *vinegar*. In my first book, *No-Hassle Housecleaning*,

I showed readers how to keep their homes clean in three easy steps. If you've read it before, you know that I'm a very outspoken advocate of these two natural cleaners. If you haven't read it, well, here's my opportunity to share a few of my favorite cleaning secrets with you!

Sure, there may be times you'll want to reach for a bottle of commercial cleaner, or maybe you just can't be bothered with anything but the brands of cleaners that you've come to know and love. But, if you keep a good supply of both baking soda and white vinegar on hand, you'll likely never be stuck in a cleaning situation that you cannot scrub yourself out of again. And, from a purely frugal frame of mind, using these and other natural homemade cleaners are just as easy on your wallet as they are on your lungs.

Kitchen and Bathroom

These are two heavily used zones in your home, and therefore can be the most difficult to keep tidy. All those meals and snacks in the kitchen, and showers and hours of beautifying in the bathroom add up to big messes. Keep the mess managed by learning to pick up items as soon as you're finished with them—a particularly important rule to teach to your children. (Learn to P.A.Y.—pickup after yourself!) A simple bottle of Very Vinegar cleaner will clean most surfaces well—about one part white vinegar to four parts water, with a little squirt of natural dishwashing liquid. Give the spray bottle (a nice clean one, please, that never contained chemicals before) a shake and then clean to your heart's content. Plain vinegar and water is perfect for mirrors or any faucets, as is flat or fizzy club soda.

Baking soda is a great cleaner to scrub the tub and leave it sparkling. If you find it difficult to get in and clean all the nooks and crannies, find a long-handled scrub brush to take off some of the pressure. Or, try my trick for cleaning the tub and shower—just scrub it clean while you're in there taking a shower! Keep a little scrubby pad in there for that purpose and take a couple of minutes to scrub away while your conditioner is making your hair magnificent. Do this on a regular basis and you won't have the bother of scrubbing an entire tub ever again!

Floors

Hardwood floors look spectacular and are relatively easy to take care of. Keep them looking lovely by making sure to limit the moisture you clean them with. A very slightly moistened mop or a cloth attached to the head of a dry static mop will do nicely. Linoleum floors are easy to care for with a little soapy water and a mop, but make sure not to line the floors with rubber-backed mats, which stain the linoleum in an irreversible way. Remember that any floor surface can be cleaned with a little soapy water and a splash of white vinegar thrown into the mix. But, use a very small amount of soap or you might leave behind residue that ironically will attract and hold onto dirt.

Laundry

Fresh laundry, white and billowy and drying in the breeze—sounds lovely doesn't it? Keep laundry beautiful but less costly by:

- Using less detergent. The new front-loading machines need very little detergent to do an effective job of cleaning: ¼ cup of detergent is all it takes in those machines. In regular top-loading washers, use ½ cup of detergent instead. You can usually get by using half of what is recommended on the package and still have nice clean clothes. That way, each box or bottle of detergent lasts you twice as long.

- Save on detergent. Switching to store brands will save you about 40 percent without ever searching for coupons. Stick to liquid detergents to avoid those nasty white residue spots left behind by powder. Liquid detergents also double as a powerful pretreatment making them a two-for-one product.
- Bleach less. Yes, bleach does work to get your clothes white, but so does borax or vinegar, minus the lung-burning chemicals. About a cup of vinegar in your wash instead of bleach should do the trick. For whiter whites, presoak the clothing in hot water with a bit of detergent and a half cup of vinegar.

You aren't the hired help, right? So get your family in on the cleaning fun, and yes, I did say fun. If you aim to simplify your cleaning routines, you'll not only save money, but also time. Delegate cleaning tasks to other family members and then don't be nitpicky—be thankful that they're trying to help out. Your positive attitude will rub off and create some contagious enthusiasm, even when it comes to uninspirational tasks like cleaning the loo.

THE CREATIVITY OF RECYCLING

Recycling often invokes images of bits of junky scraps all bundled together, and not much else. Recycling in its truest sense, however, is the epitome of a frugal attitude—using and reusing everything you have, appreciating what you've got and not wasting. You don't have to go out and buy something new, because you can create something new from something forgotten that you already possess.

Think twice before you throw anything away. Many items that we consider junk could, in fact, be useful if we slowed down and let ourselves recognize their potential. Beautifully shaped glass jars and bottles are ideal containers for garden fresh flowers. Broken plates or teacups can be turned into mosaic art with a little creative flair and some mortar. (Find it at the hardware store. If you go to the craft shop, they'll charge you premium prices.)

You can create something new from something forgotten.

This matter of reusing and recycling is really more about your attitude than anything else. You need to adopt an attitude of gratitude (which is downright catchy to say, too). Since our world has developed a throw-away mentality, you might have to work on learning to appreciate even simple things. Here are some ways to show your appreciation for what you've got by reusing stuff that, on the surface, might seem like junk.

- **Cans.** Unusual tin cans from the supermarket or specialty food store are sometimes so pretty that you hate to throw them away, especially the ones with bright labels. Plant seedlings in these by drilling a few holes in the bottom to allow for drainage. Or, fill those cans with sand, and then nestle tea lights safely inside for unique candle holders.
- **Cutlery.** I've seen artisans create simple, yet stunning pieces of jewelry by twisting the tines of forks into sculptural rings,

Recycled Art = Income Potential

Your newly recycled creations might not only make you happy, but might develop a following. Many artisans make a nice additional income by selling their wares on auction sites online, or through specialty craft e-commerce sites like Etsy (www.etsy.com).

or cutting the handle ends off of spoons and flattening and then forming them into rings. Use old forks as name card holders—those tines hold name cards perfectly, and create a conversation piece.

- **Jewelry.** Even if the piece is hopelessly outdated (and some of us like that outdated look), you can dismantle it to get bits and pieces to create your own custom jewelry. Remnants of cheap costume jewelry can be reclaimed and merged to create montage jewelry that is very unique.

- **Photo frames.** Frames don't go with your room? The easiest fix is to spray them with matte or shiny paint in the color of our choice. For kids frames, provide them with add-ons, like beads and buttons, that they can attach with glue.

- **Photos without the frames.** Hang them on lengths of fishing line. It's easy to switch the photos and keep them current as you add to the collection. Use your favorite clips to attach the photos to the line.

- **CDs and DVDs.** These are all too often thrown into landfills when our music or movie collection gets decluttered. If resale is not an option, you can cut these into abstract shapes and combine with glue in interesting ways (with other little accoutrements such as beads or faux jewels) and create a 3-D brooch. (Jewelry findings can be found at dollar stores or craft stores.) The trick is to create a piece that no one would ever guess was an old CD in the first place.

KEEP THE CAR RUNNING FOR LESS

Your vehicle gets you and your family from point A to point B safely, and for some of us, that is really all that matters. For others, that same vehicle is a serious style statement, an outward show of who they feel they are inside. Regardless, we all need to limit the costs of running our vehicles if we're trying to live large on less. So, take a good hard look in the rearview mirror and see some savings speeding your way.

How to Save Money on Your Vehicle

- **Before buying.** Before ever buying a car, find one that keeps its value longer so that if you ever need to sell, you'll be able to get more money back.
- **One-year rule.** Consider buying a one-year-old vehicle instead of brand new. You'll save about 20 percent off the original price, and yet still have an essentially new vehicle. You'll also avoid the huge amount of depreciation new vehicles experience in the first year.
- **If you're buying used, don't be a naïve buyer.** Check with Carfax to see the history of the vehicle, including any accidents or flood damage. Ask for an inspection if possible or bring along a friend or family member who is car savvy when you check out the vehicle.
- **Go small.** Save up to $400 a year on gas simply by choosing a smaller vehicle in the first place. Choose a four-cylinder engine, which may not be as peppy, but cuts down dramatically on the rate you burn through fuel.
- **Maintenance.** Keeping your car well maintained is a sure way to extend its life. Get your oil checked and changed regularly to prevent avoidable repair jobs later on. Check the owner's manual that came with your car to discover how long you can go between oil changes. Always follow the manual—you can often go 5,000 to 7,000 miles between oil changes as

opposed to the 3,000 miles most quick lube places suggest. (Remember, quick lubes are a business and want customers to return as often as possible.)

- **Repairs.** Finding a good mechanic that you can trust might not always mean going to the nearest body shop. Ask friends and family for their recommendations so that you don't get cheated. Always get estimates before doing any major work, especially if it's work that is found during a routine inspection and doesn't prevent you from driving around to other mechanics. Don't be afraid to get a second opinion, especially if you don't know the shop's reputation.

- **Consider learning the basics.** Taking a night class or learning from a friend about basic car maintenance and repair can save you thousands of dollars over just a few years. Basic services like replacing bulbs in your brake lights or doing an oil change is not beyond the skills of even those of us who feel completely inept as soon as the front hood is raised.

- **Keep a record of your maintenance and repairs.** Especially if you're not mechanically inclined, you'll want to keep a record to ensure that you're not getting hosed by an unethical

Make That Garage Pay

If you have a large garage with unused space, consider renting it out by the month. People who own additional cars, boats or motorcycles are willing to pay to rent extra garage space. Check your paper's classifieds or online at Craigslist to see what the going rate is.

mechanic who insists you need to replace a part again, even though you just had it done a year or two ago.

- **Gas grades.** Your car doesn't need premium gas, but the very lowest octane might not be your best choice either. Read your vehicle's owner manual for suggestions on how low your car's gas rank can go.
- **Wash your car yourself.** Premium car washes around my neighborhood go for at least fourteen dollars. Fourteen dollars! For a car wash! Get out the bucket and hose and clean your ride yourself. It's one way to spoil your car without dousing your budget.
- **Check your tires.** Low tire pressure can reduce your car's fuel efficiency. Again, check the manufacturer's suggestion in the car manual that came with your vehicle for the best tire pressure. For every pound of pressure your tires are under inflated, you can lose up to 5 percent fuel efficiency.

Your home and car have never looked better! And, best of all, they're looking fabulous while keeping your budget firmly in mind. You're proof positive that real style and elegance doesn't need to come with a hefty price tag attached.

SPENDING CHALLENGE

1. **Energy savings.** Everyone wins just by participating. The money you save on your electric bill goes into a jar or savings account for something the entire family wants. A vacation, a trip to the zoo or a nice night out at the movies. Keep track

of the savings to prove to your family how much they're helping by being more aware.

2. **Gas savings.** See how long one tank of gas can last. Combine trips to conserve your gas and drive as little as possible. Choose a lower octane gas to further your savings.

3. **Reuse it challenge.** Take an object normally destined for the trash can and give everyone a few days to think of a useful way to reuse the item. The best idea(s) wins! (The reward shouldn't cost you a thing—examples are a night off from doing dishes or getting to choose which TV show is watched that evening.)

6 | Big Eats on a Low Budget

Let's set the record straight: The most delicious food is also a great value. So, if you think that a low-budget lifestyle means that you're going to live on macaroni mixes and cardboard-esque frozen pizzas, think again. Frugal food is a foodie's dream come true because it's fresh, wholesome and real.

Cutting back on your overall food costs can add up to incredible monthly savings, allowing you to pay off debt or accomplish other goals you set in chapter one. As far as variable expenses go, food costs are way up there. So, chopping these expenses will mean a huge reduction in overall spending. I'll give you tons of tips and ideas for mastering supermarket savings.

But groceries aren't the only food cost you need to worry about. Those meals out and pricey lattes add up fast and can ruin your budget. I'm not saying you can never eat at a restaurant again. I simply want to show you how to treat yourself to occasional meals out. The bonus being that those evenings out will actually feel like a treat because you won't begrudgingly rely on them every day. I think you're going to enjoy cooking and eating more than ever!

DINING OUT: HOW TO LIMIT IT BUT LOVE IT

Fabulous frugal living doesn't mean you'll never step foot inside your favorite restaurant again. But it does mean chopping your spending by limiting these excursions. Your B-4 (see chapter two) should include not only a slot for tracking grocery expenditures, but also a slot for eating out. Eating out means absolutely anything that you ingest that wasn't prepared at home—including take-out coffees, donuts, snacks from convenience stores and vending machines.

To stick to your new eating-in plan you'll create in this chapter, discover the reasons *why* you eat out so frequently. Is it because you're running to gymnastics class with the kids? (Then keep an assortment of tortilla wraps and pitas available to stuff with protein and veggies that the kids can eat in the car.) Do you eat out to treat yourself? (Then find new ways to treat yourself, such as watching your favorite movie or enjoying a hobby instead.) Or, are you just a foodie at heart, longing to try the best offerings? (Then take that love of food and discover your own creative streak in the kitchen. Sure, you might not be Wolfgang Puck, but you might surprise yourself.)

Even if you don't think eating out is a problem for you, try this challenge: Carefully track your eating out expenditures for an entire month, keeping your pattern as close to normal as possible. This includes snacks on the go, coffees to go, fast food and meals at restaurants. If it's not prepared at home, it counts. At the end of the month, take a look at how much you spent. This can be quite an eye opener, and provide you with motivation needed to break the cycle of dining out too often.

Point blank, if eating out is hurting your budget, then *slash* it! Get honest with yourself here and figure out exactly how many times you splurge a week, and then cut that in half *immediately*. Meaning if you usually eat out four times a week, your first goal is to slash that to only two times a week, at the same time reducing the money spent by at least half. Once you've reduced eating out, go further until you eat out only once a week. Keep going until you reach the frequency that fits your budget. Maybe you can only afford once every two weeks or only once a month.

Is It the Little Extras That Get You?

Just for you java junkies, here are some techniques to help you break the habit of dropping by your favorite coffee shops for those endless espressos. Most fancy café drinks can be easily replicated at home. Both cappuccinos and lattes begin with good, freshly brewed espresso. And no, that doesn't mean you need a few hundred dollars to purchase some glamorous countertop appliance. Instead, purchase an inexpensive stovetop espresso maker. These are generally made of aluminum and are the traditional Italian style that bubbles and brews on the stovetop, creating water pressure from below that pushes the brewed espresso up past the ground beans to the top of the pot. A handheld milk frother can cost as little as a few dollars and create mounds of luscious foamy steamed milk in minutes. These simple tools, or a reliable electric coffee maker, can fill your portable thermal travel mug with delicious caffeinated treats for pennies.

If you really love drinks made fresh from the hands of a talented barista and can't stand the thought of giving them up, limit your coffee allowance to a certain amount per month. See what your B-4 budget will allow and then fill a gift card in that amount at the café and make it last the entire month. When the money on the card is gone, your trips to the coffee shop are over for the month. Also, ask friends and family members for gift cards to your favorite coffee shop in lieu of other presents.

Now, maybe coffee isn't your thing at all. It might be snacks that are killing your budget during the work week. Snack confessions, please. Do you indulge in sweet snacks like candy bars and pastries, or salty munchies like potato chips? Bringing snacks from home is far cheaper, plus you can substitute healthier nibbles, which will ease your budget and your belt. Instead of those chips, you could bring salted pretzels, or even better would be some chopped veggies with low-fat dip or hummus. Buy a large bag of veggies and when you get home from the supermarket, pour out individual portions into baggies or sealable plastic containers that you can tote to work. For snack inspiration, visit a bulk foods store and see what goodies will tickle your tastebuds but cost less per 100 grams.

To add a touch of fun, try one of the spending challenges listed at the end of this chapter. At first this will be tough, so challenge yourself and then reward yourself—with some small, frugal treat—when you stick to your allotted number of meals out for any given week. In no time, you'll look back and wonder how on earth you could've possibly eaten in restaurants so often!

Snack Attack

Instead of rushing out to the convenience store or hitting the vending machine at work, try …

- One of my favorite snacks is Italian popcorn. Pop some plain popcorn kernels and add a tablespoon or two of olive oil, a generous shaking of Parmesan cheese and Italian herbs if you like. (I usually do it without the herbs—just the cheese and oil and salt are all I need for my favorite snack.) Toss and serve.

- Smoothies! Basically blending your favorite fruits into a drinkable snack, smoothies are everyone's favorite. An amazing way to get kids to drink their fruit! Add frozen fruit, a banana, some yogurt if you like, and either milk or fruit juice. Whir it up, pour it out and drink up your vitamins. Try experimenting with different flavor combinations.

- Homemade pudding. Homemade pudding tastes so much yummier than the commercial tubs and is fun to make. Find a recipe in your favorite cookbook. Ingredients will include sugar, milk, cornstarch and flavorings (cocoa powder, vanilla, butterscotch, etc.). Add a little plop of whipped cream on top for the ultimate comfort food to dive into. The price per serving is so much cheaper than the tubs and you can use this as a cheaper alternative to ice cream.

- Peanut butter cracker sandwiches. Why buy premade ones? Seriously, it takes two seconds to smear on peanut butter and then stick two crackers together. Chocolate fiends—add a drizzle of chocolate syrup in each sandwich filling for total satisfaction. Again, the price per serving is much less than pre-made versions, and you can use your favorite brand of peanut butter and variety of cracker.

Make batches of these on the weekend and nibble on them during the week.

SLASHING GROCERY BILLS

Now that you're not relying on restaurants to supply your food, you'll have to rely on the supermarket. Grocery shopping is reminiscent of going to the gym. "Huh?" you might be asking. Well, you either love it or hate it, full stop. Some people absolutely adore going to the supermarket, taking their time to linger and browse, comparing products and finding inspiration. Then there are people who cannot stand the supermarket. They'd rather just pick up fast food to go—at any time of the day, any day of the week. That is just one reason why so many of us find ourselves in debt or struggling to make ends meet—we want the fast fix, including our food. Instead of slowing down and taking a little time to enjoy preparing and eating our food, we rush through everything life throws at us, including what we consume.

You Pay for a Pretty Store

The prettiest stores (with designer décor and matching gourmet coffee shops) are definitely going to hit your pocketbook harder. It's a sad, but true rule: the uglier the grocery store, the better the prices. Fewer frills means lower prices. When selecting a supermarket, remember that you have a lot of options, including local shops, large national chains, big box stores and membership stores like Costco or Sam's Club. For certain items, it will pay to shop at the less chic, but cheaper warehouse-type stores. To know if a bulk buy is a bargain, compare the price per unit and don't assume that larger stores always have lower prices. Take into account that the large membership stores do charge a yearly membership fee, so make sure you're getting enough value for your membership to continue renewing it.

> The uglier the grocery store, the better the prices.

A terrific way to find out which stores have the lowest overall prices in your area is to do a search online for "cheapest groceries

+ (your town name)." Frugal folks love to brag about the specials they've snagged, and you will likely find local forums where people are talking about the best prices.

Many stores are willing to accept competitor's coupons or even match prices, so ask about these policies at the customer service desk at every store you shop at. (It's a better option than asking a million questions to the harried cashier at the checkout.) To have a

Supermarket Sales Tactics

Grocery stores are in it for the profits just like any business, and they use some powerful tactics to get you to spend more. "Specials" on the ends of rows aren't always good deals at all, so take time to go compare those prices with other similar products down the aisles. Companies actually pay big bucks to have their products placed in these prime locations. Other tactics include enticing hungry shoppers to buy based on their olfactory senses: meaning that those roasted deli chickens and freshly baked loaves end up in your cart, because they smelled too good to resist. Combat that by having a snack before going shopping! And finally, stay focused, because major departments like produce, meat and dairy are always placed around the perimeter of the store, forcing you to walk through snack foods and other non-essentials. Be determined to stick to your list—another reason why that list is so important in the first place. And the store will try one more time to tempt you just before you leave the store, while you're wearily waiting in line. You'll see lines of products to tempt you, from overpriced batteries to bottled beverages.

price matched, bring along the flyer or clipping from the newspaper with the price and product clearly stated. Also be sure to find out which stores, if any, in your area offer double or triple coupon days—a windfall for anyone wanting to make their grocery dollars stretch further.

How to Save Big at the Grocery Store

1. **Loyalty programs.** Supermarkets want you to keep shopping with them—and only them—so loyalty programs and cards have become very popular. These are free to sign up for, and when you swipe the card when you shop, you earn points. These points accumulate over time and can be useful to redeem for free groceries or other small gifts or rewards. Be sure to sign up for these cards at every supermarket you shop at. Make sure to shop the specials and don't overspend just to get the rewards.

2. **Calculate the savings.** Bring your calculator to keep track of actual spending. Keeping a small calculator in your handbag all the time or using the calculator on your cell phone will make this easy, and you'll find it becomes a challenge to spend less!

3. **Essentials vs. extras.** Buy essentials first. If you have eighty-five dollars to spend, it'll be of more value to have purchased food essentials like produce, baking supplies and meat, not extras like air freshener. If you find it easy to get distracted, mark essentials on your list with a highlighter and get those things first. Then, see what extras—if any—your budget will allow. Shop for those luxuries only after you have purchased all of your essentials.

4. **Checking out the check out.** Ooh, can you say temptation! There are loads of impulse buys here to avoid. If you get easily swayed, grab a magazine while you wait in line and browse the articles until you're up at the cash register, and then leave the magazine behind.

5. **Compare package weight, not the size.** Items are often over packaged, and you end up paying for extra packaging, not extra product. Check the weight of products and per unit pricing (price per 100g or 100 ml, etc.) to see what is truly a better bargain. Bigger is not always better; sometimes, a smaller package on sale is cheaper than the price per unit of its larger counterpart.

6. **Don't fall for their ploys.** Clever supermarket ploys are meant to make you break your budget! Everything from the layout and design of the store, to smells of fresh bread baking or coffee brewing are all meant to entice you to spend. Once you're aware of these ploys, you'll be more resistant to them. You're no sucker.

7. **Coupons plus sales.** Yes, you can use coupons on sale items! And not only money-saving coupons, but "buy one, get one free" coupons, and "buy this, get that" coupons (for instance: buy a box of cereal, get a jug of milk for free).

8. **What your eyes see.** The items placed at your (and your children's) eye level is not a fluke! These are carefully chosen pricier items that will get you to spend more. So take the time to scan the shelves, knowing that the bargains are more likely to be found above or below eye level.

9. **Get real and eat real.** Real food is simple food. Apples. Cucumbers. Butter. Cream. Bacon. You get the idea. Rely less on

mixes and prepared foods and make stuff yourself. You may not believe this is cheaper, but compare the price per volume and see for yourself.

10. **Enlist a list.** Even when you only need a few things at the store, take a list! And then, stick to it. For large shopping trips, lists are essential and will save you lots of dollars. For quick trips, they will save you time, help you stay focused and help you avoid impulse items.

11. **Reduced meats.** Ask at the meat counter for the days when meats get marked down and shop on those days to get up to 50 percent off on perfectly good meal builders. This meat is typically close to its sell-by date, and while it is still good to eat, you need to cook it or freeze it within a day of purchasing it or it will spoil.

12. **Groceries at your door.** Some online grocery services are worth it, especially if you find it hard not to impulse buy. For new moms especially, these can be a real blessing.

13. **Past-best produce.** A slight bruise here or there doesn't mean it's hopeless! These veggies are delicious in soups, stews or sauces. Overripe bananas are just aching to be mashed and used in loaves and muffins—or to be whirred into your favorite smoothie to add nutrition and substance. Check out the produce section for a discount bin containing these veggies and fruits; they're often half the regular price.

14. **Try me free offers.** Watch the shelves for these amazing deals; they're basically the opportunity to purchase the product and then get fully reimbursed by sending in a form and proof of purchase. It's a great way to try out new products, risk free.

15. **Double coupon days.** A valuable coupon doubled makes an

undeniable deal! Ask about the coupon day schedule at the customer service counter of your grocery store, and keep an eye peeled in your local papers for these special savings and mark the date on your calendar. Aim to use your best coupons on these double coupon days—you'll walk away with some incredible bargains.

Generous Generics

The bland, singularly colored, generic boxes, cans or packets of food just don't look as tempting as those gorgeously designed packages of brand name foods. If you're used to buying those pricey standards week after week, you might really miss grabbing what's familiar. And, you might insist that the generic brands just don't taste the same and certainly aren't the same quality.

But, in reality, you're getting exactly the same type of food for 30–40 percent less. Did you know that many generic products are manufactured in the same building as the brand names? It's true! So, if there's not a great sale on the brand name (which can bring the price even lower than a generic), then head for the boring, but oh-so-budget-friendly generic brand. Give it a try, you brand snob, and you'll be happy you did. Your B-4 will certainly thank you.

The Pitfalls of Pre-Made

A good rule of thumb to keep in mind while shopping is that more convenient items will hit your pocketbook harder. In the produce section, packages of pre-chopped and washed salads are definitely an easy grab for dinner, but they'll cost far more—sometimes three times as much. Any individual-sized serving of food from potato chips to carrots will cost more than a larger bag. To get maximum value for your buck, stick with stuff you'll need to peel, chop, slice and rinse yourself. It'll only take a few minutes, and over time, these seemingly minute savings really add up.

Eagle Eyes for Sales Signs

Frugalites the world over have the ability with one quick glance to pick out every sale or clearance sign in their immediate vicinity. Utilizing grocery sales can take a little research, either by getting fliers delivered to you in your local paper or viewing such fliers online for free. Either way, with continued use and research, you're going to be able to determine what a real sale is and when it's the right time to stock up. A price book will help you do this with confidence. A price book is a way to keep track of the prices you are paying at the grocery store. Take a notebook with you when you go shopping. Write down the date, the store and the exact price and size of the products you buy. After a few trips, you'll be able to compare actual prices so you'll know when a price is a real deal or not. And when it is, you can stock up on it until the next sale rolls around.

Another trick is to keep your eagle eyes peeled for clearance sections in your supermarket. (Or anywhere at all that you shop.) These sections are where the retailers place the "final notice" goods—stuff they want off the shelves to make space for new stock. These sections are usually full a day or two after a holiday, and you can get the holiday-themed products (such as candies, cookies and grill-out items) for at least 50 percent off. I've purchased swanky bath and body goodies for ninety-nine cents that were originally over fifteen dollars each this way! Once you know where the different clearance sections are (and there can be one in each of the major sections), keep an eye open to see what goodies are offered.

THE REASONABLE COUPONER

As amazed as I am by some inspiring frugalites who are able to reduce their overall grocery bill by ridiculous amounts—sometimes 75 percent or more!—I'm also sure that for most of us, the idea of getting so into couponing isn't reasonable. To save that much money, you need to invest serious time to find all those coupons and research the deals. I'd like for you to find a happy medium when it comes to coupons. Your time is just as valuable a resource as your moolah, after all. And as you get more and more adept at finding the real sales, not the contrived ones, you'll discover that you can save an awful lot of money even before you retrieve a coupon from the Sunday papers, just by using smarter shopping techniques.

Remember that coupons can be used on sale items in almost every chain store, and many local stores honor competitors coupons. Ask about the store's coupon policy at the customer service desk before you start shopping; that way you're not surprised in line when you already have all your items out of your cart. If the store doesn't have a good coupon policy, shop somewhere else.

Where to Find Coupons

Right, so you love the idea of using coupons, if only you could find the blasted things! Here's where to look:

1. **Newspapers and flier inserts.** Contact your local papers and ask them when the coupon inserts will be included. If you find amazing coupons in an issue, it might be worthwhile to buy a few copies to stock up, particularly if they're free product coupons. (And, if you check fliers online, you can get the actual coupons when you go to the store—fliers are usually located near the entrance.)

2. **Shelves at supermarkets and discount stores.** Pads of coupons or coupon dispensers can be found on the store shelves. Take a few extras for later on, or to share with a coupon pal.

3. **On the products.** Little peelable coupons can sometimes be found right on the product.

4. **On the back of receipts.** Sometimes coupons can be found right on the back of your receipt once you've paid for your groceries!

5. **Coupon groups.** A fun and free way to find and swap coupons! Online (or snail mail) coupon groups allow similarly minded frugalites to share their coupon bounty.

6. **Product Web sites.** Almost all products have a Web site written on their packaging. These sites typically have coupons and

Living Large Tip: Watch Them Ring It Up

Watch carefully while the cashier is ringing in your purchases. If an item rings up at a higher price than what was on the shelf, you might be in luck. (Your price book will help you check for errors.) Many retailers voluntarily reimburse you if you've been overcharged, up to a certain price limit. Most people just don't know about this, but it can save you hundreds of dollars a year, since these mistakes happen frequently. Ask at the customer service desk if this is a policy of their store. (In Canada, this is called the Scanning Code of Practice.) Then mention this policy when you are overcharged, and you might get the product for *free*! It is also a good idea to double-check your receipt before you leave the store to make sure no items were accidentally rung up twice.

even giveaway offers. Check your favorite brands' Web sites often. The site will also have a "comments" or "contact us" section. Try writing an e-mail to your favorite companies, telling them your positive experiences with their products. To promote customer loyalty, these companies will sometimes send out coupons as a thank you. On the other hand, if you've had legitimate problems with a certain product, letting the manufacturer know about your complaint may end up netting you some valuable—even free product—coupons. You can also address these concerns using the phone number printed on the packaging.

7. **Swap with friends.** Tell everyone to keep an eye open for coupons when they're out doing their own shopping. This kills two frugal birds with one stone, since they'll provide you with coupons and, when they see how much money you're saving, they'll want to start couponing too!

8. **Coupon Web sites.** A search for "coupon Web sites" on a search engine will quickly net you thousands of results. These can be very worthwhile. Coupons.com is the largest and easiest to remember, and on any given day, they generally have a selection of over a hundred printable coupons you can use at any grocery store in the U.S., covering all types of products like food, health and beauty items or baby necessities. Search through these Web sites to find more coupons for your stash and keep in mind that you should never have to pay to receive any manufacturer's coupons.

9. **Specific Web searches.** If you have a product you love using do a quick internet search of "(product name) + coupon." This helps you find coupons you know you'll use.

Finding a Home for Coupons

A mini accordion file folder makes it easy to store your coupons. Some are made specifically for coupons, with special labels already printed. Some people prefer a small photo album, so they can see their coupons at a glance. Since we're keeping this couponing thing reasonable, you'll likely find that something small enough to keep in your backpack or handbag all the time is the best choice. That way, you'll have your coupon stash available any time you really need it—like when you see a great sale that will be made even sweeter with that one dollar off coupon!

While you should usually never have to pay for coupons, there is one notable exception. Large, localized coupon books that are often sold to raise funds for charities or organizations can be obtained for thirty to fifty dollars and house hundreds of valuable coupons. These coupons range in category from restaurants to hotel savings and coupons for local attractions. The largest of these is the annual Entertainment coupon book, available www.entertainment.com. When you use a single two-for-one coupon at a nice restaurant, you've already made back your investment, so this book could help you stretch your dining out and entertainment budget further. You can view local coupons online to see if it's worth your while to invest the money before you buy.

GROCERY LIST AND MEAL PLANNING

It doesn't matter if you're single or feeding a family of six, you need to plan meals and then make grocery lists with that meal plan in mind. It works to cut costs dramatically for every family and every situation. I know, I know … I hate planning, too, but I've learned the hard way that it's the only way to keep on budget. If you don't have a plan, you'll waste money. And waste doesn't taste good, no matter how you slice it. So, here goes …

Meal planning means sitting down once a week to figure out what your family will eat for the entire week. Sort of logical, right? This includes breakfast, lunch and dinner every day. For breakfast and lunch, I keep it pretty generic. For example, for breakfast you have a choice of toast, oatmeal or cold cereal with fruit or yogurt on the side. For lunch: sandwiches, soup or leftovers. See, not as complicated as you thought. If you have money in your B-4 for eating out, include that in your meal plan for the week. For dinner, some people keep it simple and have a theme for each night. For example: Monday is Homemade Pizza Night; Tuesday is Pasta Night; Wednesday is Breakfast for Supper Night, etc. Try that out for a week and see if it works for your family.

Some of us are a little more free spirited with our meal plans, preferring to try out new recipes and ideas all the time. So, do what works for you—themed meal plans or not—it's all good. As long as you sit down once a week and figure out the meals for that week, you're ahead of the game. I do my meal planning every Sunday because that's when all the new grocery fliers are published. I can see at a glance what the great sales are and plan my meals around those sales. You'll see a *huge* reduction in grocery prices from that alone!

The Three List Grocery Plan
Planning your meals and groceries basically boils down to having three lists on hand. That's not so overwhelming, right?

1. **Ongoing grocery list.** Keep a pad of paper on your fridge at all times. As you notice that you're running low on something—not when you've already run out—jot down that item. This way you'll never run out of the important items that make meal and snack times easier. Ask your family members to also jot down these items.

2. **Meal plan list.** This is basically your meal plan—a menu for the week. If possible, keep this on the fridge as well, or somewhere easily seen in the kitchen. You can switch around meals according to what you or your family feels like that day. You'll have all the ingredients on hand, so swapping around a meal here or there is no biggie.

3. **Supermarket grocery list**. This is the actual list you'll take with you when you go grocery shopping, compiled of items on your ongoing list, items to make the meals on your meal

Learning How to Cook

Sounds daunting, doesn't it? But if you don't know how to make basics, then learn! Absolutely anyone can learn how to cook. Get a good cookbook for beginners and watch cooking shows on TV to get accustomed to basic techniques and build on your knowledge. You'll pick up skills in no time and impress family and friends with your culinary swagger. (I can honestly say that most of my cooking know-how came from watching the Food Network, and now I love to cook! If you don't have cable or satellite, public television stations have a large lineup of cooking programs you can enjoy for free. You can also find video demonstrations online.)

planner list and items on sale. Divide the list into major categories such as produce, pets, and frozen foods to make it easier to shop.

No More Dinner Dilemmas: Fab, Frugal Mealtime Inspiration

So, you're already making a meal plan every week, but to make those delicious, healthful meals for your family that also means you need to get cooking. If you're already a chef-in-training (right at home in the kitchen stirring, sautéing and filleting), then bravo! You can likely skip this section altogether. If, however, you're intimidated by the idea of cooking meals regularly, this section is devoted to you.

A Nicely Packed Pantry

When pantry essentials like flour, rice, pasta sauce or oats are on a fantastic sale, stock up. Doing this week after week means you'll soon have a pantry filled with stuff you can use in a pinch to whip up easy meals, therefore reducing the temptation to nip over to the local burger joint for a quick double cheeseburger. Here is a basic listing of what your nicely packed pantry should contain:

1. **Baking supplies.** Including baking soda and powder, vanilla, and other must-have ingredients like cornmeal and bran.
2. **Canned soups.** Check for lower sodium varieties; these are a good fast meal on their own with some cheese toast and salad, or can be used to create casseroles. Go for generic or store brands unless the name brands are on special for less.
3. **Canned tuna and salmon.** For sandwich fillings, or to add some protein to any meal.
4. **Canned veggies.** Including tomatoes, which are a mainstay in any pantry.

5. **Cereals.** Cold cereal is an absolute must—the ultimate frugal breakfast or snack.

6. **Crackers.** Ideal little snackers, or crush them to use as coating for chicken or fish or to replace breadcrumbs in recipes.

7. **Beans.** Dried or canned, whatever you find easier to use. The dried varieties will cost less, but take longer to prepare.

8. **Flours.** All-purpose, whole wheat, etc. Store flour in the freezer to prevent unwelcome visitors like weevils. Seal the flour tightly in a plastic bag to keep the flavor fresh.

9. **Nuts and nut butters.** These are mini protein powerhouses! Nut butters are delicious spread on bread or crackers or added to baked items.

10. **Oats.** Delicious as a hot breakfast cereal or added to hearty muffins and cookies.

11. **Oils.** Olive, vegetable, flavored—whatever you like to use.

Bulk Up With Lentils

You can bulk up ground meats with a handful of lentils. Depending on the dish, this can fool most anyone and is very filling. It works great in pasta sauces or anything slow cooked—just don't overdo the fillers, and your family will never notice any difference. In slow cooking sauces like pasta sauce, the lentils will cook just fine as you simmer the sauce. Otherwise, use precooked (or canned) lentils. The cooking directions will be included on the package for the different varieties of lentils, but generally you need to boil them for a few minutes and then let them simmer until tender.

12. **Pasta.** The quintessential frugal meal foundation—add sauces, veggies or meat to your heart's content. Keep a good variety of pasta on hand all the time and you'll never have to run out to get a fast-food meal. (Pasta sauce is also a must have for your stocked pantry.)

13. **Rice.** Brown and white, possibly Arborio rice if you enjoy whipping up batches of risotto.

14. **Vinegar.** Vinegar has a good, long shelf life, so stock up when it's on sale. White vinegar is useful for cleaning (see page 106); specialty vinegars, like balsamic or red wine vinegar, are delicious in main dishes and in homemade salad dressings.

15. **Spices.** Not an absolute must, but who wants food with no flavor? At the minimum, keep extra salt and pepper on hand, garlic powder and something with a little heat, such as hot red pepper flakes.

Fresh Grown Frugality

Whether you have a tiny balcony or a rambling back yard, you can grow some fresh produce to supplement your weekly shopping. Containers are perfect for growing herbs, tomatoes, lettuce or berries. If you have a big green space to play with, go crazy! Ask gardening friends for advice on getting started. They'll likely also be happy to provide you with some seeds or seedlings to start.

If you really aren't into the idea of gardening, or your lack of outdoor space prohibits it, see if friends or family members would be willing to share the fruits of their gardening labors. There are always too many tomatoes or zucchinis for one family anyway, so ask if you can help out in the garden and then get "paid" with some fresh veggies. Besides, gardening is a fun and low-cost activity that also happens to reduce stress. So, don your gardening gloves and start digging.

Five Fresh Foods Frugalites Favor

Whew, try saying that ten times! Obviously, grow the veggies that you and your family will really enjoy and eat. Beyond that, here are five veggies that have maximum impact on your meals. They also are inexpensive and have longer shelf lives then most fresh veggies.

1. **Carrots.** Carrots are a great staple veggie to have on hand. They can be: grated and stirred into cakes, cookies or muffins; grated, for a fast and easy salad with some mayo, a handful of raisins, and sunflower seeds; cooked and jazzed up with fresh ginger, and a bit of honey and butter; or, peeled and sliced into sticks to take for snacks—to work, school or to tote on long drives.

2. **Apples.** Keep a bag of apples in the fridge all the time. They're healthful and portable little snacks, plus they're perfect for baking. Apples are wonderful in pies, muffins, cakes, cookies and even grated in pancakes.

3. **Lettuce.** The basis of any good salad; it's nice to be able to go get a fresh lettuce from the ground for your dinner salad. Try some interesting varieties for added color and texture. Whole heads of lettuce are much cheaper (and often fresher) than the prechopped bags of salad. Clean and chop the lettuce as soon as you get home from the store so you can make a salad or top a sandwich whenever you like.

4. **Onions.** While rarely a main vegetable dish, anyone who loves to cook probably can't imagine culinary life without onions. Red or green onions bring a milder onion flavor to salads or

sandwich fillings, while the heartier yellow onions add real punch to everything from soups to pasta sauces.

5. **Potatoes**. Potatoes are a frugalite's friend! Turn them into:
   - Mashed potatoes to top a meat or veggie pie.
   - Homemade french fries. Scrub the taters, slice them into sticks or wedges, drizzle them with olive oil and plenty of salt and pepper, and bake (turning often) at 400°F (204°C) until they are tender and crispy.
   - Herbed hashbrowns. Toss diced potatoes with olive oil, salt and pepper and bake until cooked through and browned. Add a big handful of chopped fresh parsley at the end—great for brunch.

"Raid the Pantry" Meals (No Money Meals)

Payday is too many days away, and you need to feed the family with stuff on-hand in the freezer, pantry and fridge. I know you're feeling stressed, so first things first, make a list of absolutely everything you have on hand. This is when you'll be relieved that you stocked up

Grow Your Own Herbs

A handful of herbs adds flavor and brightness to any dish, from pasta to soups. Sure, they're not the basis of a meal, but they make any meal much more palatable. Plus, it is so much cheaper to grow your own herbs than reach for those overpriced packets in the produce department! Window herb garden kits let you grow your own herbs all year long no matter where you live.

on essentials when you had the chance (and money) to. Casseroles, soups, stews or pasta dishes are high up on the No Money Meals list. A can of tuna will add essential protein. Baked goods are an easy, frugal treat—homemade oatmeal cookies, cakes or muffins with whatever stuff you have on hand to throw in.

Twenty Ideas to Get Your Culinary Creativity Flowing

1. **The beanery.** Eating beans makes you … ummm … digestively happy even if those around you aren't quite so thrilled! Beans are a mainstay of any frugal diet, and they're not as boring as you might suspect. Add beans to soups, casseroles or just about any dish in place of meat. (Vegetarian chili, for instance, is so rich and delicious that you'll never miss the meat.) Rich, baked beans are divine, and perfect with a chunk of homemade bread and a light salad. Black beans bulk up a salsa or salad and can even be made into burgers.

2. **Eggs-actly a meal.** Keep a dozen eggs in the fridge all the time. Not only necessary for many homemade baked goods, these essentials are the basis of light meals like omelets, frittatas or scramblers. (A scrambler is a combination of eggs and bacon or sausage, all atop a layer of hash browns. Delicious!) Hard-boiled eggs are quick and easy sources of protein and are great in salads or on sandwiches.

3. **Hooray for casseroles.** A frugalite's favorite meal, since there will usually be plenty of leftovers to freeze for later or eat the next day for lunch or dinner. Search for recipes that use your favorite ingredients for a casserole that you'll love.

4. **Garden fresh.** If you've got a green thumb, then you're on the path to major food savings. Fresh veggies like zucchini,

tomatoes and lettuce are all easy enough for beginners to
grow. Use seeds for ultimate savings. Focus on growing veggies that will save you the most—things like sweet peppers
can be pricey at the supermarket, so growing your own will
save you big bucks.

5. **Never ending salad bowl.** One great big green salad is the beginning of so many incredible meals. Add grilled chicken, fish
or beef and a tangy dressing for a main course. Or, add sliced
hard-boiled egg, strips of cheese or cooked chickpeas for an
easy lunch on the go. This applies equally well to fruit—keep
a bowl of fruit salad in the fridge, and as you finish off the
fruit, add more so you have a healthy dessert any time.

6. **This is corny.** Cornmeal. Grits are gorgeous! And good for
you, and, oh right, did I mention cheap? Cornmeal is also
a nice addition to your regular pancakes, adding flavor and
fiber to boot.

7. **Griddle my cakes.** Pancakes and crepes can be made more
interesting with additions like fruit, chopped nuts or cottage
cheese. (Cottage cheese pancakes are so good! Find a recipe
online to try.) Fill the plate, add extra fruit and maple syrup
and thrill anyone sitting at the table.

8. **Leftover heaven.** I love leftovers! Take any leftovers—and I do
mean anything—and turn them into something else entirely.
Leftover meat is easy to chop and add cold on top of salads,
as sandwich fillings, or to soups, casseroles or pasta sauces.
Leftovers are ideal lunches the next day.

9. **Home-baked café.** I'm a fan of easy, portable snacks and
breakfasts. And having them in hand means you won't stop
at some drive thru. Muffins can house all the goodies of a full

breakfast in one cute little cakey confection. Add chopped nuts, berries, grated carrots or a handful of chocolate chips and you have an instant classic. Homemade granola bars are healthier and less sugary. And what can I say about brownies? It's another fun, frugal treat (especially if you use cocoa in place of baking chocolate). Make brownie sundaes with a rich gooey brownie as the base, then add ice cream and toppings. Bliss in a bowl!

10. **Pasta, pasta and more pasta.** Any type (whole wheat, rice pasta for you gluten free eaters like myself, white pasta) and any shape should be lining your pantry at all times. Grab a package of pasta to make the easiest meal ever: Simply combine cooked pasta with olive oil, herbs, salt and pepper, steamed veggies and lots of Parmesan cheese. Toss and eat. So simple, so delicious and so very frugal. And it tastes just as good cold as it did hot.

11. **Particularly poultry.** When chicken is on sale, stock up; it's the core of many homemade meals. Whether your specialty is fried chicken, barbecued chicken, chicken casserole or chicken fajitas—poultry is a must-have. Buying the pieces, such as legs or thighs, is cheapest. But, if your meal prep is rushed, then wait for the skinless boneless breasts to go on a fantastic sale and stock up and freeze them. It's still cheaper if it means you'll be eating at home.

12. **Recreate it!** Take your favorite take-out or restaurant meals and recreate them at home. If you're a food whiz, you'll likely enjoy this experimentation. Search the Internet or the library for copycat recipes. It'll cost way less and will likely be lower in fat and salt.

13. **Rice riches.** From main dish to side dish to sweet endings, rice is a serious multitasker. Brown rice costs more, but is a whole grain and therefore healthier. You can use brown rice in the same ways as white; it just takes longer to cook, so plan ahead. Rice pudding is the ultimate creamy comfort dessert, with lots of cinnamon and raisins.

14. **Your daily bread.** Fresh loaves of home-baked bread are enough to make anybody salivate and reach for the butter dish. Basic loaves are easy to master, and, if you have a bread machine, they're ridiculously simple. The cost is very low—buy bulk jars of yeast to cut down on the priciest ingredient. Get creative with additions such as grains, seeds and flavorings.

15. **Sir sandwich.** It's not just for tuna salad, baby! A sandwich filling can be as unique as the leftovers inhabiting your refrigerator. Leftover roast beef, cream cheese and spring veggies, turkey and cranberries, or vegetarian sandwich slices and a pile of fresh herbs slathered in grainy mustard. Anything delicious in the fridge can become a sandwich filling, easy to tote for lunch to work or school.

16. **Skewer me dinner.** Take basic ingredients like cubed chicken, salmon or steak, add some chunks of veggies (peppers, zucchini and mushrooms are some of my favs), marinate them in your favorite salad dressing and then grill. Easy and gourmet! Plus, you'll use smaller portions of meat and veggies because everything is chopped up.

17. **Soups and stews.** If you've never made soup, you're in for a treat. Soup is basically some main ingredients—maybe chicken and veggies—a broth component (it can just be water or canned chicken or beef stock) and some flavorings.

That's it. Simmer them together in a nice big soup pot for as long as you can to bring all the flavors together, and you have a downright tasty meal. Soups and stews are great to make in a slow cooker.

18. **Spice is so nice.** Add a dash of heat in the form of hot sauce to just about any boring old dish for instant appeal.

19. **Sweetie treats.** Homemade candies and fudges are beyond fabulous! From easy to make cocoa truffles to decadent fudge with nuts, this is a great way to treat your family occasionally, for not a lot of loot. A carefully created box of candies or fudge makes a beautiful gift, and basic recipes will only set you back a few dollars for a huge batch—way cheaper than the chocolate in the candy aisle.

20. **Try tofu!** Give me a chance here! If you buy extra firm tofu and marinate it in some lovely bright flavors—like ginger, lime juice and garlic—it takes on the flavors like a sponge. You can bake or sauté the tofu cubes in a little oil. Or, add soft tofu to homemade smoothies for a boost of protein that is heart healthy *and* cheap. (Take that, you overpriced protein shakes! We have something better and more natural.)

Ten More Ways to Save on Food

1. **Food or baking swap.** Get a few friends in on this and swap a main dish once a month. You'll have to make a few casseroles, but you'll get some interesting new meals in exchange. The same rules apply to a monthly baking or cookie swap.

2. **Once a month cooking.** Do the majority of your cooking for the month all in one day! Find books at the library for inspiration, ideas and recipes. It'll take a lot of effort on that day,

but think of the freedom of grabbing meals from the freezer on busy nights, knowing they're homemade and healthy.

3. **Trade and barter.** Your friend has too many zucchinis and you have too many tomatoes. Telling people what you have an excess of will get them talking about their own gardening efforts, and the next seamless step is to swap excess fruits and veggies. This also applies if you bought a mega bag of flour and need to exchange some for something else.

4. **Bulk buying.** Stock up on items you use all the time and in great quantity. Always check the price per unit to see if it's a true bargain. Resist the temptation to buy huge quantities of things you don't need.

5. **Leave the kids at home.** Or your spouse if he or she is a spendaholic. You'll have your own challenges to stick to your list and stay on budget without your family sidetracking you.

6. **Pay with cash.** Unless you get valuable loyalty points with a credit card. (I think those make it worth it, if you pay them off immediately.) Using cash makes you more aware of true spending and forces you to stick to the budget you created.

7. **Careful coupons.** Sure, you did save seventy-five cents on that four dollar item. But would you have saved two dollars by buying the store brand instead? The lowest price is your aim, not just the bragging rights to say you used a coupon.

8. **Beverage dilemma.** Freshly squeezed juices are always more expensive than the juice boxes. Try making your own fresh squeezed juice at home. And forget pricey bottled water— drink tap water or try a filter pitcher to improve taste. If you love soda, stock up on cans when it's on sale and carry a can to work instead of getting one from the vending machine.

9. **Meaty meals.** Large frozen packages of meats are budget friendly compared to "air chilled" meats. This applies to skinless, boneless chicken breasts, or burgers and steaks.

10. **Find a farmer.** A local farmer might provide you with fresh chickens or beef or pork or fresh eggs and produce. Ask around, and check at a local food co-op for information.

SPENDING CHALLENGE

1. **No-dining-out challenge.** For one week or one month, you choose! You'll see how much you can save, and you'll learn that eating at home is always the frugal option. And you'll get mucho creative in the kitchen.

2. **Shop at home challenge.** Instead of automatically running to the store for the ingredients of your favorite recipe, shop inside your own pantry, refrigerator and freezer to find stuff you can throw together to make a meal. Some of these impromptu meals are the most satisfying, and you didn't spend one extra red cent!

3. **Waste not, want not challenge.** For one week don't throw out any food whatsoever! Statistics show that we throw away up to 30 percent of our food—a staggering amount of waste. Make it your goal to use up what you have before it needs tossing. Make plans to cook fresh produce and meat before it goes bad and eat leftovers for lunch.

7 | Live It Up and Save Some Dough

The most common misconception about a money-conscious lifestyle is that it's horribly boring. Some people reason that there's no room for good times while responsibly caring for money matters. Right? Wrong! We'll disprove that thinking in this chapter and give you an arsenal of ideas on how to get entertained—and be entertaining—at a price you can afford. And we'll prove that watching your pennies in other areas allows you to save up for special events and trips that you might not have been able to enjoy otherwise.

CELEBRATIONS FOR CENTS

Most any party or celebration has five essentials:

1. Location and decoration
2. Food and drink
3. Atmosphere and music
4. Captured memories
5. Gifts

Great Location and Decorations

Depending on the celebration, this will change dramatically. When choosing a location, remember that, in warm weather, most people would rather be outside enjoying the fresh air than stuck inside a room, so make the most of any pretty outdoor space you have, or reserve a pavilion at a public park. You could party in your backyard or on the roof of your building or balcony (if you live in a high-rise in the city). If you're hosting in your own home, rearrange the furniture in your living room and other public areas to accommodate a crowd and let people move around the party. Create conversation nooks, a food area and open space for dancing and mingling.

Find inspiration for decorating your space for any season by visiting the library and checking out books and magazines on entertainment and home décor. Here are some more low-cost ideas:

- **Fresh flowers.** Pick flowers fresh from the garden in summer, and in winter, use pinecones and pine branches.
- **Lights.** Fairy lights always seem beautiful no matter what the season, and stringing them up inside or out creates a dreamy setting to make memories in. Go with white lights so you can use them any time of year.
- **Candles add a nice touch.** Buy neutral colors so you can use them for any occasion.
- **Balloons.** Save on balloons by buying a bag of them and inflating them with your own lung power. Hang them from the ceiling with ribbon (no helium necessary), or attach them to tables and doorways.
- **Get artistic and create your own decorations.** If you can't draw, find items to trace in magazines, or use stencils. Make construction paper snowflakes, falling leaves, pumpkins, etc. A

word of warning—you can spend more on homemade decorations than on store-bought ones if you buy all-new supplies to make the decorations. Plan not to spend any money and just use what you have around your house—markers, printer paper, old wrapping paper, tape, glue, etc.

Great Food and Drink

Here are some great ideas for saving on food and drink:

- **Potluck.** Have everyone pitch in and supply his or her favorite snack or buffet item. Provide the main dish and have others provide the sides or dessert. Or have a theme—like dip night, Mexican night or fondue—and ask everyone to bring their favorite recipes.

- **Limit or eliminate alcoholic drinks.** Serve punch and soft drinks instead. Watch the savings add up.

- **Make it a tasting.** If you're worried your friends will think your party is cheap (or worse, lame) without alcohol, make it a BYOB event, but be classy about it. Tell guests the theme is wine tasting or beer tasting and ask everyone to bring their favorite bottle of wine or six pack of brew and their wine glasses or pint glasses.

- **Don't do disposable.** Make the event fancy (and earth-friendly) by using your best dishes instead of disposable. This adds a nice finishing touch to sit-down meals and doesn't cost anything other than elbow grease. If you're having a large crowd and don't have enough dishes for everyone, ask each person to bring his or her own plate, silverware and glass. It can be fun if they bring their favorite dishes, which can be a great conversation starter and the variety of cutlery could add a decorative flare to the event. Point out how not using disposable products will help the environment and no one will mind. Do be sure to have your sink ready so people can scrub their dishes up quickly before they leave.

- **Make it mini.** Miniature foods like tiny burgers, miniature stuffed potato skins or mini cupcakes are very trendy and prove that people think less is more. Plus, the mini stylized food means you'll prepare less overall, cutting food costs while still being cool.
- **Pizzas all around.** Personalized pizzas are fun and inexpensive to make, and they please just about any crowd. Make up a big batch of pizza dough (flour, a little salt, some yeast and warm water), and then pull off individual portions for each person to make their own pie. Provide bowls of toppings including tomato sauce, alfredo sauce, thinly sliced veggies, fresh herbs and of course lots of cheese! Have the oven ready to pop in the pizzas as your friends finish creating their masterpieces. The best part of all—no one can complain that they don't like the food because they created it themselves!

A Punchy Beverage

My favorite punch, which I discovered by mistake, is: two cans of frozen fruit punch concentrate, a two-liter bottle of ginger ale and plenty of ice to fill up the punch bowl. It's a perpetual favorite, and the ingredients are budget friendly.

Great Atmosphere and Music

Beautiful music changes the whole feel of a get together. Here are some low-cost ways to add that atmosphere:

- **Live music.** Know a friend who plays violin or classical guitar? Ask them to play for you and barter for their services, or just feed them really well and provide them with delicious leftovers to take home.
- **Dance music.** Need music that inspires a crowd to dance? Look online for the top dance hits of any given year and find tunes that everyone will be boogying to. They won't be able to help themselves.

Great Memories, Captured

Any true celebration needs to be captured in photo or video form. Digital photography cuts out much of the expense of traditional photography because you can pick and choose exactly the photos you want printed and the duds can be deleted. Digital video cameras are a great option if you prefer your memories in motion, just be sure you will use the device enough to justify the purchase. Many cell phones and digital cameras also offer a video setting, so you don't necessarily have to run out and buy a video camera.

Great Gifts

Amazing gifts are heartfelt ones that you give to the people you really care for. They're the gifts that the recipients keep for years because they made such an emotional impact on them. And thankfully for us frugalites, those are also the kind of gifts that can be made, not purchased. Even if you don't consider yourself very crafty, you can make some simple homemade gifts that will be very appreciated.

Theme Me Up, Scotty

Sometimes you just want a reason to party, so pick a theme to liven up the festivities. Some ideas are:

- **Hawaiian.** Wear the tackiest tropical shirt you can find, and even socks and sandals if you're feeling crazy. Tiki torches add great mood lighting and keep mosquitoes away for a low cost.

- **'80s Night.** A great excuse to tease your bangs sky high. Free (and funny) decorating idea: Ask people to bring photos of themselves from the '80s and tape them all to a posterboard when they arrive.

- **Around the world.** Explore favorite travel destinations and nibble on local specialties. Ask guests to bring their favorite ethnic dish.

- **Sci-fi.** Die-hard fans always have a theme near at hand, complete with complicated handshakes and pointy ears to be worn. Hey, it's your party, so it's all good.

- **Cook-off.** Pick a dish or an ingredient (such as corn, pumpkin or egg plant) and ask guests to bring their best version.

- **Tacky holiday.** Make it a contest to see who can show up in the tackiest holiday attire (it can be any holiday). For free decorating, ask guests to bring the tackiest decoration they can find. Thrift stores are gold mines for both outfits and decorations.

- **Fan boy (or girl).** Cheer on your favorite team with face paint and jerseys. Ask guests to bring their favorite tailgate dish. Not a sports fan? Celebrate your favorite TV show or movie.

- **I'm a celebrity.** Have guests dress up as either their favorite celebrities or the celebrities they most resemble. Or, get guests to dress up as celebrities and have the others guess who they are. The guest with the most correct answers wins!

- **Gift baskets.** Specialty baskets can easily cost upwards of a hundred dollars or more. But, you'd be pleasantly surprised by what you can accomplish with about twenty dollars, or even less if you already have a collection of basket-worthy goodies sitting around the house. And you don't have to put the items in a basket. You could use other containers, such as a hatbox, a planter, a colander for food items, a bucket or a fashionable gift bag. Dollar stores are a treasure trove of basket additions—search out the good stuff among the junk.

- **Hand-knit or sewn items.** I remember a beautiful quilted bag my aunt made for me that was simply the perfect gift. Even as a teenager, I loved going to the library and loading up with books, and that bag often made the trip with me. Keep the recipient in mind—it seems like you can never go wrong

Low-Cost Costumes

Sometimes you need a costume, but it can be tricky to find a budget-friendly getup. First, visit secondhand stores where you can find amazing costume elements for a few dollars, especially items like retro clothing to create a disco diva or nerd ensemble. (Hint: The shorter the pants, the more authentic the nerd!) You may even be able to find actual costumes, depending on the season and store. Dollar stores stock elements like face makeup or hats, and sometimes kids' toys work well to add a touch here and there. Know a friend who wears a uniform at work? Borrow it and become a nurse or policeman for the evening and be impressively authentic.

with something like a cute hand-knit scarf or mittens, or a beautiful bag, or throw cushions to match their décor.

- **Unique art.** The kids can help out with this one! Who can resist a piece of artwork by a budding artiste? Certainly not an appreciative aunt or grandpa! Get the kids to help create a gift, then frame it in a discount store frame. By providing your children with similarly sized paper each time, they can refill that relative's frame with new art whenever artistry strikes them.

- **Jar gifts.** The Internet is littered with ideas on creating mixes or other types of gifts poured neatly into jars. I've seen many of these offered at farmer's markets or craft sales and they always sell, so they're definitely popular. These mixes can range from hot cocoa or mocha mixes to homemade cake or biscuit mixes to bath mixes. Bath salts or body scrubs are perfect in sealed Mason jars, and the ingredients for one batch will make plenty of jars, so for one price, you can whip up a lot of gifts. (Always make extra, and keep these gifts ready to give at a moment's notice whenever you need one, such as for a small hostess gift.)

- **Pet gifts.** Nothing impresses someone more than remembering their beloved pet with a little gift all its own. Dog or cat treat recipes are easy to pull together—most call for some type of protein (like meat or eggs) and grains such as oats. You could even try your hand at making custom-made pet toys such as catnip bags or squeaker toys.

- **Cheaper greeting cards.** While undoubtedly lovely, it's hard to swallow the five dollar price tag on many greeting cards. Either stock up on greeting cards at the dollar store or check on eBay for large lots of cards for cheap. They're usually last season's selection and have to be taken off the shelf to make room for new stock.

- **DIY greeting cards.** If you don't like the look (or cost) of commercial greeting cards, make your own! Blank cardstock cards are available at some dollar stores, around ten to twenty of them for a buck. Or, make your own cards by folding cardstock. Paint a design or paste on a picture or go crazy with creating your own style. If you're not artistic, make a card on your computer. Personalize it by including your own photos. Envelopes can be had for cheap—or nothing at all—by asking at local card shops. Sometimes they'll gladly give you a box of extras for free, just to get them off their hands.

Ten Freebie Gifts

For when the budget can't budge even a little to provide a gift, here are the ultimate gifts that won't cost you a cent.

1. **Gift cards you already have.** That gift card to your favorite coffee shop or restaurant can easily be regifted and passed along to someone else. Just make sure they weren't the original gift giver, and you should be fine. Unused cards are ideal, obviously. But if the card is for a business that lets you add money to gift cards, and you still have a reasonable amount left on it, take it back into the store and add enough money to it get it up to an even amount (such as $25 instead of $22.43) so it's like an unused card.

2. **Natural gifts.** Go out in the backyard and see what beautiful things you can gather together into a creative bouquet. If you have artistic flair, this shouldn't be too hard. Put it all

together in an oversized glass and finish it off with any type of ribbon you have to loop and make a bow. You can also pick up bits of nature while you are on vacation. Save these as gifts for special occasions or let them be souvenir gifts.

3. **Garments Rethought.** A funky, old scarf that you haven't worn in years can be cut up and turned into a one-of-a-kind throw pillow for a friend. A bright sock that's missing its mate can be stuffed and sewn into an entertaining hand puppet for a child. Recently, I even saw old, lacy bras that had been transformed into gorgeous evening bags! (That made me laugh—it truly proves that nothing needs to ever be thrown away.)

4. **Your own jewelry.** You might have a pretty piece of jewelry that you haven't worn in ages, but that would look great on your friend. Retro jewelry is the coolest, and since you already own it, you won't have to shell out to provide a gift for a pal. This is another opportunity to create jewelry from pieces you already have and can re-envision.

5. **Raid the storage area.** If you were a big shopper in the past, you may have unused new items—home décor stuff, makeup or perfume—still lingering in your closets. Those make perfectly good gifts.

6. **Freely wrapping.** It's astonishing how much specialty wrapping paper can set you back. Add a ribbon and bow, plus a card, and that really adds up! Use your imagination to come up with alternatives—like newspapers, stylish fliers, take-out menus or cool package linings from food items. If you insist on something more traditional, the dollar store is again the best source for wrapping paper for a cool buck.

7. **Gifts from the heart.** Ask any mother if she would love to

receive a beautiful letter from one of her children, and you'll
get a resoundingly positive reply. A letter thanking someone
for all they've done for you or poetry that you've written
yourself is sure to be appreciated and probably tucked away
for safekeeping for a very long time.

8. **Foodie Gifts.** Need a gift for a foodie? Take a serious look
through your cupboards and see what mixes, sauces or exotic
foods you can spare. Or, maybe you never used that kitchen
gadget you were so taken by—add that to a little foodie gift
basket for your friend.

9. **No more wine-ing.** A nice bottle of wine is always a perfect gift.
If you have a collection of bottles, you won't really notice that
one bottle is gone. Giving a gift of your favorite wine is even
nicer if you add a little note explaining why it's your favorite
or when you first enjoyed it.

10. **Coupons with practical value.** Don't have a cent to spend on a
friend? Create a booklet with a few coupons for services you
can provide, such as an evening of babysitting at no charge
or a fresh batch of your famous homemade cookies. This is
an especially good gift idea for those recipients who already
have everything; we all know how tough those people can be
to buy for.

DREAM VACATIONS MINUS THE DEBT

Sure, an overflowing wallet makes travel easier, but it certainly
doesn't make it superior. Armed with some professional traveler's
tips, you'll be able to create the kind of getaway that is just right for
you, and easy on your B-4 budget.

1. **Collect travel miles and points**. So far, by collecting travel miles,

my husband and I have gotten a free car rental and reduced flights. And we haven't even been collecting for long, plus we don't spend that much! Be careful to research which programs are worth joining and which are useless. Keep your program cards on hand all the time, so you can always collect your points.

2. **Sign up for bargain travel newsletters online.** To be among the first to hear of great deals, you'll need to sign up for travel newsletters online. Some are compilations of the best deals from a variety of different airlines, hotels or travel agencies— all of the best bargains collected in one convenient location. Those are the ones to sign up for, and they should always be free. Expedia (www.expedia.com) and itravel2000.com will send you periodic e-mails with their very best deals on the locations you're interested in. Cheapflights.com has a free newsletter they send out with the best deals on flights.

3. **Check out travel magazines.** Subscriptions to those beautiful, glossy travel magazines are expensive, but well worth checking out from the library for free. This way, you can discover which places you'd like to visit and create a dream list to work with. Armed with that list, go online to see what bargain options are available for those areas.

4. **Go low, go long.** Low season is the peak time to travel for frugalites! My husband and I make a point of travelling during the off-season. If you don't have kids, then you, too, have a lot of flexibility to travel when your money will stretch further. And stretch further it will, since off-peak rates for popular vacation destinations can be half the peak season rate. If you book your trip for right before or right after the

peak season, you'll still enjoy the nice weather and sights without dealing with higher prices or large crowds.

5. **Swap houses.** So, you have a place in the U.S. and Marilyn has a sweet little cottage in the south of England. Every day, people all around the world swap houses for vacationing. Check out sites such as The Vacation Exchange Network, www.thevacationexchange.com or Homeexchange.com.

6. **Visit *en famile*.** Family members living in lovely places are an easier and cheaper destination. Remember, though, that frugality isn't miserliness. Make sure to keep your stay pleasant for everyone by providing groceries if needed and a thoughtful thank you gift at the end. And, of course, offer to have them stay with you whenever they like.

7. **Stay in an condo or house rather than a hotel.** By renting an condo or house during your vacation, you'll feel like you're really living there, not just visiting. The cost is usually far less than a hotel suite. Search online for "vacation rentals + (the area you'd like to visit)."

8. **Dining out vs. dining in.** Another benefit of renting a condo rather than a hotel suite is having a small kitchen, which allows you to make at least a meal or two every day at your home away from home. Even if you do choose a hotel suite, select one with a mini fridge and microwave. That will allow you to have some simple breakfasts in your hotel room at the very least. Every meal that you can prepare yourself (even if it's cold cereal and milk with fruit on the side) will save you a ton of cash. Another bonus of a good hotel is free continental breakfasts! Eat your fill and then face a great vacation day.

Visual Vacation Reminder

Keep a cutout from a travel brochure of your next vacation spot and stick it on the fridge, or right on your wallet if that will help prevent impulse buys. When you're craving a shopping trip, that small picture will remind you that it's either the retail trip or the actual trip, but it can't be both.

9. **Stick to a daily vacation budget.** Keep your notebook handy. On a typical vacation day, you'll likely be spending more than you would normally at home. You'll have a set budget for the trip, so use a notebook to track spending and stay on budget. If you have a spending-mad day, make it your determination to ease up on the cash outflow the next day. Or give yourself a per diem and stick to it. That will be the easiest way to stick to your budget.

10. **Challenge the family.** Ask your family what activities they most want to do and then challenge everyone to find ways to do as much possible while remaining within your budget. Not only does this make money-saving more fun but it also makes everyone accountable for spending. It'll be a reality check that vacationing doesn't mean a spending free-for-all.

Save ... and Then Travel

Stress-free vacations are those that you've already paid for before you travel, so plan way ahead. Don't get caught in the common trap of plunking the entire cost of the trip onto the handiest credit card, figuring that you'll pay for it later. All that does is add to your debt load, and it certainly doesn't make for a relaxing vacation. Instead, sit down and figure out how much money you'll need for this trip—for car and gas, travel tickets, spending money, accommodations, food and miscellaneous. Always include a miscellaneous category, since unexpected expenses are sure to arise, you might as well expect them.

Once you have the budget estimate for your trip, start saving toward it. Put a little something in your trip savings fund whenever you get a paycheck or receive money (such as a gift, or by selling something). In a notebook or spreadsheet, keep track of the date, the amount of money added, where the money was from and your new total. I also like adding a percentage of the total amount needed to keep me motivated to continue saving. Again, get the family involved in this part of the trip, too. A few dollars here or there from your kids will help the grand total edge up and will teach them how good it feels to give toward something they really want. To raise additional needed funds for your vacation, hold a family garage sale, sell some stuff you don't need on eBay or take on a few extra shifts at work.

EVERYDAY FRUGAL FUN

Some of our most precious childhood memories are those times that seemed like ordinary occasions on the surface, but looking back, they were extraordinary because of the people or places we were enjoying.

Forty Fun Frugal Activities

1. **Taking photos.** A creative pursuit anytime. Any reason is a good reason to take out the camera.

The Snacks Are Gonna Get You!

It's not just the meals that add up so outrageously when travelling, but the coffees, beverages and snacks! Before heading out, stock up on some favorites like granola bars, teas, soda and bottled water. Here's one example: I bought a twenty-four-pack of spring water for $1.99 before going on one trip. When I checked the hotel vending machine, one bottle cost two dollars! So, in essence I got twenty-four bottles for the price of one. Love that!

2. **Fishing.** Love it or hate it, but if you get into it, this is not only an incredibly peaceful way to spend some time, but also a handy way to stock the freezer with fresh catches.

3. **Treasure hunts (geocaching).** Geocaching is the modern version of the treasure hunts we enjoyed as kids. This time, you're searching for real buried treasure, left behind by another geocache fan. All you need is a GPS unit (borrow one from a technically-knowledgeable friend) and to visit the official site at www.geocaching.com.

4. **Hiking/walking.** Go on an urban hike throughout your own city or town and discover previously hidden gems. Or, get out of the city and go on a real hike, complete with a backpack slung over your shoulder.

5. **Sightsee like a tourist at home.** Search for tourist sites in your own hometown and find some amazing things to do near home. The goal is, of course, to find frugal activities that also teach you something.

6. **Reading.** Always a popular activity around my house, a good book can be had at the library for merely an annual renewal fee (or free if it's a municipal library). Or, check out second-hand book shops for old favorites.

7. **Writing.** Ever since I first learned to write, I have loved writing down thoughts, ideas and dreams. Your writing might be for publication or it might be entirely for your own consumption. Regardless, writing is a frugal and heartening activity you can enjoy any time, anywhere.

8. **Movie night.** This doesn't have to cost a cent. Keep track of when good movies are playing on TV or check out a movie from the library or swap movies with friends.

9. **Artistic.** Sing, or paint or act. Do something artistic that satisfies that desire for artiness.

10. **Dance.** Dance lessons can be expensive, so get a video instead and dance somewhere with mirrors so you can tell if you're progressing. The goal isn't to be a pro, but rather to learn a new skill and have fun doing it. Are you already a funk-master on the dance floor? Then turn on some music already and get down with your groovy self.

11. **Call a friend.** An unexpected call to an old pal out of the blue will not only make his or her day, but yours as well.

12. **Memory walk.** Get out the old photo albums. Your kids will probably get a kick out of seeing what was going on in your life before they ever came on the scene. And they can make fun of your big, bad hair of years gone by, which is always guaranteed entertainment.

13. **Visit a beach.** Get outdoors for a while! Step away from modern gadgetry and enjoy being outdoors, breathing in fresher

air. Take time to really see what's around you—the trees swaying in the wind or the waves rolling up to meet the sand. This is a great way to relax and be disconnected for a while. (Yes, that means turning your cell phone off, but I know you can do it!)

14. **You pick, we pick.** Pick some produce! If you know someone who needs help picking some produce, offer your assistance. Or go to a pick-your-own-produce farm and pick apples, cherries, strawberries, pumpkins, blueberries and more. The produce will cost less, and you can ensure you get the best quality. Kids love this!

15. **Cook with care.** Many family meals today are rushed affairs, just a quick gobble before rushing out the door to the next planned activity. Give yourself some culinary breathing room and plan a nice meal that is more involved than one you'd normally prepare, and then enjoy each step. Keep your culinary aims limited to a budget you can readily afford.

16. **Visit a gallery or museum.** Take time to look and learn. Like a field trip for grown-ups.

17. **Go to a park.** Green parks are a beautiful place to visit with the family. Take a Frisbee, a bat and baseball or some old bread crusts to feed the ducks at the pond. It'll cost you nothing, but provide you with lots of fun.

18. **Decorating do-over.** Completely makeover one space in your home simply by moving furniture around and reorganizing stuff you already have.

19. **Do a fondue.** Melted chocolate. Need I say more? If you're craving some fun time with friends and family (and they happen to have a sweet tooth), this is an instant winner. You

provide the chocolate, and they can provide fresh fruit, cubes of pound cake, marshmallows and pretzels to dip into the blissful concoction. Fondue pots can cost as little as ten dollars and do a great job of keeping the chocolate molten. You can also use cheese or oil if you crave something savory.

21. **People watch.** When I have time to, I love watching humanity flow by. Perch at a good spot, like your favorite coffee shop or a park bench. There's not a single time that I'm not intrigued by at least one person, for any of a hundred reasons.

22. **Camp.** Find a favorite spot and pitch a tent for a cheap getaway anytime. Or, pitch that same tent in your backyard, and your kids will think you're amazingly cool.

23. **Take a tour.** Call around local factories and see if they provide tours to the public. You'll be surprised by how many do, and it's always educational. Often, it's also free or will snag you some free goodies.

24. **Genealogy.** Find out all about your family tree. Once you get started, you'll be hooked.

25. **Start a scrapbook.** Scrapbooking supplies can be very expensive, so stay away from the craft store and use crafting supplies from the dollar store instead. Searching on eBay can also net you cool scrapbooking stuff for a fraction of the full retail price.

26. **Solve a puzzle.** Word puzzles, jigsaw puzzles or sudoku, it's up to you. They're a great way to spend a day when the weather outside is rotten. Get jumbo activity books at a dollar store.

27. **Make a family survey.** Come up with a long list of questions and then see how well you know your family! It's a great way to encourage communication.

28. **Go on a long walk.** Go out with the dog or walk someone else's! If you don't have a dog of your own, "borrow" one and get some exercise.

29. **Wander through a grocery store.** Take your time and uncover new foods (great ones can be found in the ethnic sections) or new ways to use the stuff you already have. Often, the produce department has free recipes using different types of fresh fruits or veggies. Grab a free sample (or three) of foods while you're wandering to keep your strength up. High-end grocery stores often have wonderful samples and exotic foods. Just be sure you don't get caught up in the moment and buy a lot of things.

30. **Learn a new word and use it.** Some people like to learn a new word every day. If words are your thing, give it a try and see if it boosts your brain power.

31. **Learn how to say hello in a few different languages.** Impress people by saying "hi" in their native language. They'll be pleasantly surprised.

32. **Declutter.** This is fun for only certain types of people, I admit. If you love organizing, enjoy some free time by sorting out an area in your home.

33. **Comfy couch vacations.** Watching travel shows on TV is a great way to see the world from a truly comfortable perch. The same holds true for travel books and magazines you sign out from the library. This is travel at its very cheapest!

34. **Collect rocks/shells/butterflies.** Collecting is a relatively inexpensive hobby. You might even be able to find items in your locale that you can sell and make a profit from online.

35. **Play board games or cards.** The game could be intellectually

stimulating like chess, or just greedy fun like Monopoly. Keep some games on hand and utilize them once in a while.

36. **Start (or join) a book club.** A book club allows you to dig deeper into your reading and discuss with friends. Always check the library first for the books. The classics are typically always available for check out, and most libraries do a great job of keeping up with current titles, too. If you can't find a book you need at the library, find used copies online or at a secondhand bookstore.

37. **Go for a drive.** A little day trip is easy on the budget, and if you live near some pretty scenery, a day away from home is like a vacation minus all the hassle and fuss. Bring along beverages and snacks from home to keep the spending really low.

38. **Make some music.** Anyone musically inclined will tell you that playing music makes her heart sing. If you have an instrument or two, have a jam session with friends, or work on writing your own new material or practice a new technique to improve your skills.

39. **Take in the amateur theater.** Local schools have at least one big production every year in their drama department. Indulge in some cultural enlightenment for less and support a school.

40. **Volunteer.** Giving to someone else who really needs it is a wonderful way to spend some of your spare time. You'll meet new people, share new experiences and realize all over again how much you truly have.

Frugality means you develop an attitude of gratitude and that most certainly includes great times spent with those you love most. It's the memories from such times that are priceless, not how much you spent on any gifts or decorations.

SPENDING CHALLENGE

1. **Dreamy do-over**. Research a dream vacation and come up with a final cost. Then, research all over again to find lower cost options for each category of the trip, such as transportation, accommodations and entertainment. If you pull in the reins and are willing to save for a while to get there, you may still be able to go to your dream destination without breaking the budget.

2. **Change it up gifts**. It's pleasantly surprising how quickly change can add up to an impressive sum. Instead of spending it purposelessly on endless cups of coffee, collect it in a small jar. When it's time to purchase a small gift, you'll have some extra money waiting for that very purpose. (Tossing in a few dollars now and again will help your gift fund grow faster, so don't limit yourself to change.) Then, get creative and see what you can buy with your gift fund jar.

3. **Near and far**. Come up with two vacation options—one a faraway getaway and one nearer to home. Get the family in on the researching to come up with a final cost for each one. Make a list of pros and cons for each vacation and plan how you'll save up the money for whichever one you decide on. Before you go, research activities that are either free or low-cost so that you're not stuck with unexpected expenses once you get there. Planning the whole trip out as a family will also teach your kids that nice vacations don't just appear, but that everyone has to help in order to make them a reality.

8 Great Style and Beauty for Less

Can I tell you a little secret? It's a secret that a lot of people won't really want you to be privy to, namely people who make their livings by creating or selling clothing and jewelry, and definitely not those pesky shoe-shop owners with their gorgeous window displays that render us speechless (and just a little bit in love). Okay, this highly guarded secret is … you can look absolutely incredible for a *lot* less money than fashion insiders would have you believe. (That includes you, Stacy and Clinton, from *What Not to Wear!* How I would love to see them shop at a thrift shop … just once!)

Ladies, this first section is more for your attention, because we tend to be the more prolific shoppers. But, guys, I haven't forgotten you. You'll find shopping tips more to your liking on page 182.

Developing your very own personal style matters more than being slavishly hooked on every trend that comes along. You can be stylish and downright adorable on a fraction of what brand-name clothing costs full price. The truest style mavens can take a cart full of bargain finds and turn them into an amazing outfit with just an accessory here and draped scarf there. Add a dash of attitude—which, might I add, costs nary a cent—to pull the look together.

Whether you carefully shop sales, try out thrift store shopping or even get creative with swapping and bartering, you're going to reduce your overall clothing and accessories spending by up to 50 percent! Breathe deeply. I promise that I don't expect you to forego indulging in a cute pair of shoes every once in a while, but you will learn how to acquire those cute shoes for less.

Full retail prices—be gone! But your sales sticker cohorts are wholeheartedly welcome. Now, come along on this bargain finding journey with me to discover how fun frugal shopping can be. You'll learn that frugal fashion means being more resourceful and creative, rather than impulsive and credit-card dependent. First, though, let's talk about the tricky shopping habits that you need to identify in order to conquer consumerism.

FIND YOUR SPENDING HOT SPOTS

As with the other areas of your budget, you need to discover where your hard-earned dollars are really going on fashion items. Take out your handy B-4 budget and get honest with yourself. The reason this is such a vital step is that the actual amount we spend on non-essentials is far different than the amount we *think* we spend. (Ahhh … self delusion is so sweet.) Sure, we can admit that our mortgage or rent payments are pretty hefty, but what could we possibly spend on little extras like nail polish?

Full retail prices— be gone!

Quick, if I asked you what you spend on clothing, accessories, shoes, makeup and other beauty products and services in a month, what would your answer be? Fill in here, please: $_____.

Now, look back on credit card and debit receipts (online banking makes this a snap). What was the true cost? Where did you spend it? For many women, this is a spending hot spot, especially for women who are in the workforce. You likely feel the pressure to look good and feel that you deserve the indulgences after a hard week of work. Or, for incredibly busy moms, you feel you need a treat after the unpaid business that is motherhood.

Which of these are your spending hot spots?

- Clothing
- Shoes
- Accessories and jewelry
- Makeup and beauty stuff
- Nail care (manicures and pedicures)
- Spa services

For guys, your grooming costs might include:

- Haircuts
- Gym membership or personal trainer

Or all of the above? Yikes! It's a real eye opener, isn't it? Remember, when your budget won't stretch to allow it, *don't go to the store (or salon) in the first place!* The shopping techniques and tips that follow in this chapter are for the times you have cash in hand to pay for those items. Don't get back into the dreaded habit of rationalizing—as you grab for one of your credit cards—that "I'll pay for this next payday." Often, next payday doesn't make it in time. So, keep your spending hot spots in mind and stay away from the shops, even thrift shops, unless you have actual cash you can afford to spend in your wallet. See page 37 for more help on resisting impulse shopping.

SERIOUS STYLE WITH SERIOUS SAVINGS

Strengthening Your Frugal Fashion Core

Sounds like an excruciating workout video, doesn't it? But, when I talk about strengthening your fashion core, I mean those foundation pieces that you'll rely on time and time again to look great. These are the pieces that will easily mix and match or stylize with accessories to completely change the overall look. Think of these items as an investment. They should last you for years, so make sure they fit fabulously and have classic cuts and lines that span the fashion seasons. Department store end-of-season sales are great times to pick up these core items, but racks are often picked over at this time. Avoid this by shopping at season preview sales, often tied to a holiday at the start of a new season. You can get good deals at this time and find exactly what you want because the stores are fully stocked with new seasonal merchandise.

At the core of your closet:

1. **Great little black dress.** This is a cliché in the fashion world. But, some clichés only exist because they're truthful. That dress can look professional with a cropped jacket and a patterned scarf and sensible shoes for work. But later that evening, the jacket can come off, some more dramatic chunky jewelry can be added and some oh-so-*not*-sensible shoes can be added into the mix!

2. **A few well-fitting classic skirts** (with or without matching jackets). Pairing different blouses and tops can create entirely different looks. Change things up even more with the addition of colorful scarves and jewelry accessories. Discover which skirt styles flatter your shape and stick with what works.

3. **A summer dress or two.** Add a little shrug over the top for when the evenings get cool. This is another dress-up or dress-down basic.

4. **A few pairs of trousers.** Make sure they fit you well and are flattering. Wide-leg will suit you if you're bottom heavy; a more tailored pant will suit you if your legs are thinner.

5. **A fantastic white button-up shirt.** Classic with blue jeans. You'll look like you fit right in with the yachting crowd. Or, pair it with a great pair of trousers or a tailored skirt, or wear it loose and long and cinch it with an eye-catching belt.

6. **Two or three pairs of well-fitting jeans.** Ha! I know that finding jeans that really and truly fit properly can be a chore, but it's well worth trying on loads of pairs to get ones that make you look fantastic. You'll love wearing them.

7. **A few sweaters.** Ones in neutral colors will match just about anything. Those that are splashier will add a burst of color to your other neutral pieces—like black slacks and a black T-shirt with a bright green sweater. Choose sweaters that fit your curves, not oversized ones that fit like potato sacks.

8. **Shoe basics**. We're talking pumps, cute flats, sneakers and sandals for summer. You probably already have those in your closet right now, so next time the urge to shoe shop hits, do a reality check and shop your closet.

Now that you've examined your core, try this experiment: What items do you have in your closet or dresser *right now* that you could use to change up the look of a simple, classic black dress? A white, button-up shirt? How many total outfits could you make from that one simple foundation piece? Five? Ten? Good job, frugalista! Now you're getting the point of accessorizing to stylize basic core clothing

Reasonable Seasonables

Shop the end of season sales for at least 40 percent off good quality clothing, especially larger ticket purchases like winter coats or boots. So what if it's last season's look? Last season's look will look fabulous with your own fashion twists liberally applied.

pieces. The next time you get the urge to update your wardrobe, go to your closet instead of the mall. Spend an afternoon trying on the clothes and accessories you already have. Create new outfits, experiment with mixing and matching. You likely have far more options than you realize. Freshen old items by adding new elements, such as buttons or trim. As you mix and match, try on your clothes. Set aside the items that don't fit or don't make you feel fabulous. If these items are in good shape, you can swap them with a friend or sell them at a consignment shop.

Super Scrimper Clothing Tips

(For when money is as tight as those skinny jeans in the back of your closet.) Okay, time to get down and dirty with the frugal tips now. You need—not want—a new piece of clothing. But, your bank account and wallet are screaming for mercy. There's just not much left after the essentials have been covered. These are the ultimate frugal tips for finding new (or new-to-you) clothing that will fit the need—and you—beautifully all at the same time.

1. **Free: Help a friend "declutter."** Swoop in for clothing freebies when your friend goes on an organizing binge! This is a great

way to score fantastic new clothes for free. She'll be thrilled to get rid of closet clutter, and you'll score new swag. Be sure to return the favor the next time you declutter your closet.

2. **Free: Queen swap (not shop) a lot:** This is one of my all-time favorite ways to get great new clothes for free. Invite some buddies over for a clothing swap. Be sure to tell them to bring their old accessories too—shoes, handbags, costume jewelry, scarves—to round out the assortment. Add in coffee and treats and it equals a fun night in with the gals, while replenishing your wardrobe for nada.

3. **Free: Look out, it's a closet raid!** Whether it's your mom, your grandma or Auntie Ruth, you'll be surprised by how much cool vintage stuff can be had. Ask permission (good girl) and then raid their closets to see if you can find any cool new garments or costume jewelry for absolutely nothing.

4. **Free: Ask for a gift card.** Got a few gifts headed your way? Whatever the occasion, don't be shy about *asking* for gift cards! Let friends and family know which stores you'd most like to shop at.

5. **Cheaper: Glorious garage sales.** Maybe this doesn't strike your fancy, but you can find some fabulous items (sometimes brand new) for literally a buck or two. This is an especially great option for shopping for children, since kids grow out of clothing faster than our next craving for chocolate comes around. Ultra cheap tip: Wait until the end of the day when the garage sale hostess is ready to pack up all of the unsold stuff and tote it back inside. Then barter away!

6. **Cheaper: Thrift store sales.** Yes, even thrift stores, already known for being a penny pincher's best clothing resource,

Secondhand Spy

Buying secondhand clothing requires a little investigation. Used trousers very likely have shrunk and used shirts may be stretched out, so don't trust the sizing on the label. Try them on if possible, or, at the very least, hold them up to your body to ensure the fit. Check to make sure there are no holes or damage to the garment and ensure that the clothing isn't stained or smelly. I know this is an indelicate subject, but you don't want to be stuck with a garment that you'll never wear. No matter how cheap it was to start with, it's still overpriced if it ends up abandoned in your closet.

hold sales! Call your favorite thrift shops and ask when they are. One of my favorites has a "garbage bag" sale occasionally, where ten dollars will buy all the clothing you can fit in a large garbage bag! Look for shops that offer good quality clothing at truly affordable prices. Scour their stock regularly to find treasures. Sometimes you'll score swanky brands for way less than at a consignment store. Develop an eye for what is outdated and what is relevant now; also what you can incorporate with pieces you already have. Not all thrift stores are equal. You may need to visit several before you find one that is well organized and has a quality selection. Don't let a bad experience at one thrift shop turn you off to all of them.

7. **Cheaper: Flea markets.** For a few bucks, some flea markets have new T-shirts and other basic clothing available or even old jewelry for just twenty-five cents. Be prepared to barter!

8. **Cheaper: Dollar store diva.** True, you won't find a great outfit at a dollar store, but the interesting accessories you can find will surprise you. Keep an eye open for accessories, flip flops or sun hats that will only set you back a buck.

9. **Cheap: Online shopping.** Online auctions such as eBay have a plethora of amazing bargains to be had. You can do a search according to lowest price first and then search specifically for the items and brands you want. Be sure to get exact measurements to ensure a good fit. If the item is in used condition, keep in mind that it could well have shrunk since it was originally purchased. If you're concerned about that possibility, purchase only new clothing.

10. **Cheap: Bargain stores.** Maybe big bargain stores like Walmart don't make your heart go pitter-patter … yet. Take a closer look at the shoes, clothes and accessories (not to mention make-up and beauty supplies) at your local bargain department store. Don't be snobby—give it a try! These stores are especially good places to buy fad pieces that will be completely out of style next year and so are not worth the investment.

Online Coupon Codes

Many merchants' Web sites offer you an opportunity to insert a special money-saving code at checkout to reduce the cost of your purchase. To find those codes type in: "(store name) + coupon codes" on any search engine. Often, you can also use a coupon code on sales items. A double whammy of savings!

Clean Up With Consignment Shop Sales

Sounds too good to be true, doesn't it? Declutter your closet and walk away with a few hundred bucks? Consignment stores are an excellent way to make extra cash, but you'll need to know a few hints before you get started. First, hunt to find which consignment stores you'll sell to, and which season of clothing (spring, summer, fall or winter) they're currently accepting. Higher-end consignment stores are looking for the best quality items, and some only carry designer brand merchandise, but these spots also reap you the biggest profits. Regardless of which consignment shop you partner with, the clothing you present should look as neat, new and cared for as possible. Launder the clothes, carefully press them and fix any minor repair issues like sewing on buttons. When you go in with a load of clothing, be sure to read the fine print on the contract you'll sign, including how much percentage you'll earn on the sale and what happens if the clothes don't sell. It's pretty standard to earn 50 percent of the purchase price, so if the prices are lower than that, you might want to look elsewhere.

11. **Cheap: Consignment stores.** An excellent resource, especially if you find one that is reasonably priced. (Some of the upper echelons of consignment stores are mucho pricey!) Remember that these are a great way to earn some moolah on your nice used clothing, too.

12. **Cheap: Discount department stores.** These stores take regular-priced overstock merchandise from department stores and sell it for about half the price. You can get some name brand items. To score über deals, check out the clearance sections.

13. **Cheap: Outlet stores.** Outlet malls and shopping centers can save you a whole bunch of money. These are the shops where last seasons' merchandise goes, which means you can stock up on still-fashionable, brand-new clothing for a fraction of the price. The price reductions are very impressive, often more than half off. I've even seen 80 percent discounts (which yes, did make my heart go pitter-patter). I won't name names, but there's one lady in my family who makes a fashionable killing every time she visits the outlets in Florida, and the lower the price goes, the happier she is, as any good frugalite should be. Not sure where the outlets are located in your area? Search online for "outlet shopping + (your hometown)" to find some locations.

14. **Cheap: Clothing sales.** Nothing strikes joy into the heart of a frugalite like a fabulous clothing sale. But don't get fooled. Crafty retail merchandisers can make a ho-hum deal look spectacular with some clever signage. Remember that end-of-season sales are prime time to pick up classic pieces for reasonable prices.

15. **Cheap: Sew your own.** If you're the type who can sew a straight hem (not my forte), then sewing your own clothes is not only a budget-friendly choice, but also a way to express yourself. But if you have an eye for exquisite fabrics, sewing your own clothes might end up being pricier than just buying them on sale or secondhand. To find some beautiful fabrics at cut-rate prices, check online at eBay—you'll be surprised at the bargains to be had. You can also find some great patterns online, too. Just include the shipping charges in your overall cost. That's why this is "cheap," not cheaper.

A Closetful of Assorted Savings Tips

- **Cost per wear.** Keep track of what the item cost you, and how many times you've worn it, thus giving you a cost per wear ratio. It'll give you a better idea of the real cost (and value) of your clothing.

- **Color me lovely.** Add bursts of color or patterns to your otherwise neutral clothing for fresh looks.

- **Real vintage chic.** Accessories at thrift stores will cost pennies on the dollar compared to their pricey cousins at trendy vintage stores. Make your own vintage finds by shopping thrift shops and not those gorgeous boutiques.

- **Rethink old jewelry.** Take old, mismatched earrings and create groovy brooches. My mom is known for this. Her old, funky earrings make the coolest brooches I've ever seen.

- **Ask for a discount.** At the small kitchenware shop where I've worked for years, we often have customers asking for further discounts on items. Sometimes, with approval, we can discount an item a bit more. It's always worth asking.

- **Other Internet resources.** Whether it's free sewing patterns or ideas on how to turn that old T-shirt into a pillowcase, you'll find tons of crafty solutions online. The patterns alone will save you hundreds.

- **Web sites.** Go to the Web sites of your favorite stores and sign up for newsletters and updates, and look for exclusive coupons. These Web sites are a gold mine for hearing about the best sales and upcoming events. Sometimes they'll even have contests you can enter to win free stuff!

- **Frugal, not frumpy.** Frugal fashions that don't fit aren't flattering. Sometimes it's worth it to spend a few dollars to get a skirt or jacket properly tailored. If you love the way it fits, you'll wear it all the time, therefore getting your money's worth out of the piece. If you don't like the fit, you'll avoid wearing it. If you have a friend who's clever with sewing, ask her how much she'd charge, or barter.

- **Try it on.** Never assume that a size will fit just because it normally does. Even if a size 8 generally is perfect on you, always take time to try the clothing on. You'll see that sizes vary greatly between lines and designers and one 8 could be a 4 or a 12 in another line. This applies for both new and second-hand clothing.

- **Learn basic sewing.** A cute outfit that will last you seasons upon seasons isn't toast just because the hem is down. Teach yourself (or ask someone to teach you) how to do basic clothing fixes. Keep a little sewing kit on hand with needles, thread in a variety of colors, buttons, snaps and other assorted necessities. I'll bet your mom or grandmother would be thrilled to death to have you finally sit down and learn some sewing basics.

Recycle That Special Outfit

Make some money on that outrageous outfit you only needed for one night. If you got a great deal on that dress at a charity shop or online, clean it well and then take it to an upscale consignment store. You might not only earn back the few bucks you originally paid—but make a handsome profit!

Be Still Your Overexcited Heart: Shoes

What is it about shoes that cause us to get so terribly excited? Walking by a shoe store, we can't help but take a peek, or stop altogether and gaze with adoration at the beautiful specimens on display, all ready to tiptoe their way right into our hearts. Okay, we're going to deal with this obsession once and for all! Here are a few handy tips to save on shoes:

- **Take stock of what you already have.** Have some strappy summer sandals? Then forego this year's "must-have" pair. Already own some great black heels? Then that new pair in the store window with the cute bows attached aren't really necessary. (And, with your new resourceful frugal sensibilities, you can update your old shoes to look like the latest style, anyway.)

- **Swap shoes.** Some people are squeamish about wearing shoes anyone else has ever donned, but some of us don't mind in the least! When you do a clothing swap with friends, ask if they have some shoes to swap as well.

- **eBay.** You'll find amazing deals on exactly the shoes you want. There are even better deals on last year's styles.

- **Online discount stores.** Do a search for "discount shoes" or "shoe bargains" to find specialty discount shops online that have slashed prices on footwear. The only downer is that you'll have to pay shipping unless you can wait for a free shipping promo.

- **Shoe sales.** Any shoe shop worth it's weight in wedges has at least one or two great shoe sales a year to make way for new stock. Sign up for sale notices if they have an e-mail newsletter, or call and ask when their next big sale is.

STYLISH SAVINGS FOR THE FAMILY

As promised, we're going to focus more on you, fellas. Now is the time for tips on decking out the entire family to look their best, for less. See guys, we know it's not *all* about us. Well, not all the time.

Many of the tips already shared also apply to shopping for guys and kids. But, here are a few extra tips geared specifically toward the jocks and juniors in our lives:

For Jocks

- **Suits.** The priciest of all men's garments, the suit can be the bane of any budget. Wait for the best sales of the season, especially end-of-season sales, where you can even snag two suits for the price of one.
- **Dry cleaning.** Don't overdo it, or the prices are going to get you! Suits only need to be drycleaned two or three times a year. Maintain the suit by regularly brushing it with a good clothing brush to remove lint, hair or dust. When you do need to dryclean it, compare. Ask around for the best prices, sales and coupons.
- **Ties and accessories.** Find amazing guy's stuff online. Do a search for "discount + ties" (or whatever item you're looking for) and you'll be amazed at the savings.
- **Casual clothes.** If your guy cringes at the idea of secondhand, then you can still supply him with loads of new T-shirts for a few dollars each. Large family clothing chains (like Old Navy) have amazing weekly specials, plus online printable coupons! For jeans, khakis and shorts, always compare prices online. The Internet is a frugalite's best friend, especially if you are an easy-to-fit size.

For Juniors

- **Cut 'em down.** Not your kids, sheesh! Jeans and khakis can still be useful even after your child has sprouted, by being cut and turned into cute capris or shorts. Even PJ bottoms can be shortened and re-used if they've only grown up and not out. Get crafty and add embellishments to stylize.

- **Cool consignment.** Good consignment stores offer great merchandise and provide fair reimbursement for the kids' clothes you bring in. Ask moms in your area for the consignment stores they love, or search the local yellow pages.

- **Hand-me-downs.** Why do these have such a stigma about them? Hand-me-down clothing is a great way to save! (Even when I was a teenager, I loved getting these. Maybe I just never inherited that vital "cool gene?") So, when anyone offers you kids' clothing for free, don't even blink an eyelash before saying an energetic "Yes!"

- **Family clothing swap.** No, you don't get to swap families! But, if you have friends or family with children a year or two apart from yours, you might be able to do regular clothing swaps.

- **Sew repairs.** If you sew some of your children's clothes, make sure the bottoms have a deep hem; they are easy to let down once the kidlets start growing.

- **Rugged play clothes**. For everyday play clothes, make sure to get only budget-friendly varieties. Kids wear out clothes fast, and they grow out of them even faster!

- **Yard Sales.** Hey look, other parents are trying to get rid of clothing clutter from their offspring. This is one of the least expensive ways to adorn your kids. For the poshest kid's, brands, check out swanky neighborhoods.

- **Loyalty programs.** Take advantage of loyalty programs when you shop sales at your favorite retailer. These additional savings can add up to free stuff later on. Some retailers even have a guarantee that children's clothes won't wear out before they grow out of them. Ask your retailer if they offer this guarantee—Sears is one chain that provides this.

See, you can get the whole family looking fabulous and still stay within your budget. Your B-4 budget will thank you for such self-control and resourcefulness.

BARGAIN BEAUTY: SCORE DEALS ON HAIRCUTS, BEAUTY TREATMENTS AND MAKEUP

Anyone with even the tiniest hint of fashion sense knows that style includes a great haircut, an occasional beautifying treat and some carefully applied makeup to round out the look.

Hairstyling How-To

If you are a haircutting genius, then you've got a big edge over the rest of us. The very cheapest way to provide haircuts for your family is to cut their hair yourself. Otherwise, check out local cosmetology schools for great bargains on chic haircuts. Guys can save big bucks by keeping their hair short. A pair of electric barber clippers is all that is needed for that. Otherwise, call around and compare prices of haircuts.

For women, longer hairstyles require far less upkeep over time. Shorter dos will cost more because you'll need to pop in for a trim every month, compared to every two or three months with longer, layered styles. Here are some tips that will help you keep your locks beautiful for less.

- **Homemade hot oil treatment.** A quick raid of your pantry will provide you with a spa-licious hair treatment. Pour two tablespoons of olive oil (more if your hair is long and thick) into a microwave-safe dish or mug and heat until the oil is warmed through. Work through wet hair, concentrating on the ends. Cover with plastic wrap or a shower cap to keep in the warmth. After twenty minutes or so, rinse and shampoo out for soft, shiny hair.

> Guys can save big by keeping their hair short. For women, longer hair-styles require less upkeep.

- **Less is more.** Washing your hair, that is. Not only is it better for your hair to wash it less often, but it keeps your colored hair fresh longer. Once every other day is adequate for most people, unless you have very oily hair. Ask any hairstylist. Most follow this rule themselves.

- **Coloring hair.** Most hair coloring kits on the market leave your hair feeling silkier than before you colored! If you hate applying your own hair color, get a friend to do it. Keep in mind, if you choose a color that is drastically different from your natural shade, your roots will show much sooner and require more maintenance.

- **Prevent split ends.** And reduce the number of trims you need. Less straightening, curling and blow-drying will reduce the number of split ends you have. If you can cut out (ha ha) one or two haircuts a year, you've saved fifty to a hundred dollars or more, painlessly.

- **Get nosey.** Don't be shy, just ask that lady where she gets her hair cut! You might find out a secret hairstyling place that is also easy on the budget.

- **Try a bargain hair salon.** The décor of the salon really doesn't matter; you could save hundreds a year just by making this one change. Fifteen dollars for a haircut verses eighty-five dollars—you do the math.
- **Barter for haircuts.** Your friend cuts hair, so offer babysitting for a haircut, or mow the lawn for a haircut. Figure out what you can provide her that's valuable and then barter for your new do.
- **Get your bangs trimmed for free.** Do it yourself, or see if your salon charges nothing if you're a regular client there.
- **Go *au naturel.*** If you have curly hair, go with it and learn how to make the most of those curls. Or, if you have naturally straight hair, learn how best to style it. Endlessly fighting against our hair's natural tendencies is not only time consuming and painstaking, but it's downright expensive. (Think of those straightening or perm bills ... egads!)

Marvelous Makeup, Beauty and Skin Care for Less

I love experimenting with makeup and skin care products. It's fun to try new colors and shades, glosses and liners, lotions and gels. And while one-hundred-dollar jars of lotions and potions may claim to do everything from de-crease our wrinkles to erase pesky age spots, in reality, the most dramatic results may be our lowered bank account balances. Here's how to add up some savings while still looking beautiful:

- **Sunscreen.** Hey, I'm a redhead, so sunscreen and I have been good buddies for a really long time. Wear it daily and you'll cut down on your need for wrinkle cream and spot remover in the future. SPF 30 is the most effective. Anything lower won't give enough protection and anything higher really won't add much protection.

While one-hundred-dollar jars of lotions may claim to do everything, the most dramatic results may be lowered bank accounts.

- **Healthy skin begins with healthy food.** Mama was right—beauty really does begin within. Eating a more balanced diet will give you a healthier glow naturally. Eat less refined sugars and flours. Up your servings of fruits and veggies, whole grains and healthy fats (like olive oil, salmon and avocado).

- **Understand what looks good on you.** Even if the trendiest shade of eye shadow at the moment is lime green, you don't need to succumb. Understanding what does and doesn't work for your skin coloring helps keep makeup cravings under control. Try a free makeup session, but don't get suckered into buying every pricey "essential" used to create the look. Ask for a list of the colors used and then find a more affordable brand at a drug store.

- **Multitask makeup.** Try multitasking products that add color to eyes, lips and cheeks to keep you wallet fuller and your makeup bag clutter free. A three-in-one product will save you the cost of two other products.

- **Natural skin scrubs.** A skin scrub reveals healthier, prettier skin underneath. Use a handful of oats blended with natural plain yogurt to make a killer face mask. Or, mix brown sugar with a little vegetable oil for a toothsome body scrub that will leave skin sweet and soft.

- **Shaving cream undercover.** Use cheap hair conditioner instead of shaving cream! Slick it on, shave and then rinse. After you jump out of the shower, rub in some moisturizing lotion for smooth legs.

- **Skin cleansers.** Getting your skin good and clean (but not overly dried out) is one of the most important steps of healthy skin. A gentle face wash will work fine. Store brands work just as well as name brands.

- **Healthy, hydrated skin.** Eight glasses of water each day is the mantra we all know, but if you're working out regularly, you'll need a few extra glasses. Add a wedge of lemon, grapefruit or lime to add a bit of flavor. Or, try replacing a few cups of water with cups of herbal tea.

- **Skin loves sleep.** Easier said than done, but of course good sleep will mean you look and feel more rested. Hey, sleep is free and will pay off bountifully to make you look great. Try going to bed a little earlier than usual, and keep distractions (like computers!) far away.

- **Summertime strip down.** Less makeup, more glow. In summer we seem to peel off layers of heavy clothing and layers of heavier makeup. Forego the foundation and use a tinted moisturizer with sunblock to look great. Bronzer or self-tanners bring out the summertime glow in anyone without damaging side effects.

- **Anti-aging, anti-savings?** Anti-aging products are the costliest beauty products on the market! Don't fall for every advertiser's claim. Instead, try some of the bargain brands, and search online to see which brands people love. Often, the best aren't the most expensive.

- **Say no to smoking.** Not only is this a health no-no, but smoking also wreaks havoc on your skin. Another reason to ask your doctor for help in quitting once and for all.
- **Moisturize me, mama!** No matter your skin type, your skin needs a healthy dose of moisture to look dewy. Treat very dry skin to rich emollients like cocoa or shea butter. Skin that tends to get oily will love soaking in something lighter, such as a gel moisturizer.
- **DIY eye makeup remover.** Use vegetable oil on a cotton pad or puff. This gently and easily removes even stubborn mascara. Baby oil works great, too, and it won't leave your eyes stinging. Rinse well after the makeup is removed.
- **Super skin toner.** Pour a little witch hazel on a cotton ball and remove impurities from your skin after cleansing. Find it in any pharmacy.
- **Make yourself up online.** Check online fliers and stock up on cosmetic essentials on sale. Otherwise, this is another great time to check out eBay. Savings can be 25 percent and up, but remember to include the shipping.
- **Foot cream.** Thick, rich cocoa butter is the most decadent foot cream on earth. Slather some on your feet at night and then encase your tootsies in comfy socks. It's a deep conditioning foot treatment.
- **Beachy foot scrub.** Soften your feet at the beach *au naturel* (Hey, that's not what I meant, keep that bathing suit on!) by smoothing a handful of wet sand over your feet.
- **Specialty skin creams.** You might swear by that eighty-nine-

dollar pot of neck cream, but in reality, there's not a lot of difference in ingredients from that and a generic moisturizer. If you must have expensive creams, check online for discounts.

Whether you're a fashionable mom on the run with a row of kidlets following behind, or a single savvy lady or gent, you want to look great, but without causing your wallet to groan. Get in touch with your inner frugalista fashionista and look amazing with these tips and ideas. Once you tap into the creativity behind real style, you'll have the ammunition you need to create a fashionable look for any occasion.

SPENDING CHALLENGE

1. **No-spend month.** Now here's a challenge! For one entire month, be determined to not spend *one single cent* on clothing, accessories, shoes or makeup. Make it easier on yourself by staying far away from any tempting stores.

2. **Three revitalized outfits.** Find three outfits or pieces of clothing in your closet and revitalize or renew them. Add appliqués or new buttons, shorten or lengthen the hem, or completely redo them so they're not even recognizable. The goal is to do this for as little money as possible, so don't go crazy at the fabric store with supplies. For even more savings, try to revamp them using materials you already have, including buttons, old jewelry and old scarves.

3. **Wacky accessories challenge.** Take anything you don't need—from Aunt Millie's chipped teacup, to a retro teaspoon or a CD you've never bothered listening to—and get creative with

it! Turn that teacup into a work of wearable art. Find instructions online to turn old spoons and cutlery into amazing jewelry, or use that CD to carve out fashionable metallic jewelry for yourself or the kids. And hey, if you get good enough with creative accessories, you could always make a little more money by selling them on eBay or Etsy (a crafts shop online).

9 | Spending Less Forevermore

You've done it! You've changed how you perceive money and how you spend money, and you've discovered many ways to get the most for your money. Now that you've established a habit of saving, you want to make sure you continue this fiscally responsible behavior for the rest of your life. You know how to spend less while still enjoying the same quality of life, so why would you want to go back to overpaying? When the good times start to roll in your bank account again, you don't have to get carried away with your spending. One of the keys to continuing to live a frugal lifestyle even when everyone around you becomes money-crazed all over again is to stay focused on the reasons why you choose to save.

Remind yourself why you want to be financially responsible. Instead of spending your time searching the Web, the mall and magazines for the next hot item to buy, spend a little time perusing inspirational blogs of money mavens who manage their finances wisely. Be willing to be different, and stay that way. Look back to chapter one at the reasons you identified to start saving money. Keep these original goals firmly in mind. Goals are great tools to continue spending your pennies wisely. And a quick wander back into how it felt to be drowning in debt is another surefire way to keep firmly footed on your new frugal path.

> **Don't make the mistake of thinking saving is only for the hard times.**

Remember, if your finances are healthy, there's no reason to feel guilty for treating yourself occasionally. You might like a little extra to spend on swanky dinners or a weekend away with your beloved. Just make sure you budget for these treats and that you're getting the best price for them. The tricky thing about treats is that if they're not controlled, they can lead you back into some serious trouble. Be aware of that danger from the get-go, and make sure that treat really is an occasional event.

KEEP SAVING—EVEN IN GOOD TIMES

Don't make the mistake of thinking saving is only for the hard times. You don't have to be in dire straits financially to want to save money and to maximize your purchasing power. Make the most of every penny, even when they are plentiful. If you're wise when there is plenty, you'll be better off when lean times return. You never know when you'll be hit by a circumstance beyond your control, such as a job loss or a prolonged illness. When you do need to tighten your belt, you'll already be in the habit of it and your earlier savings will have given you a little extra to fall back on.

If this lifestyle of savings helps you rid yourself of debt, don't give up the savings practice as soon as you pay that final bill. Keep up your good habits and continue to make those payments—all of that extra money you had to devote to debt can start accumulating in savings. Shop around for the best savings accounts, those yielding the highest interest. If you have still more to play with, you might want to meet with a financial professional for advice on careful investing. As each debt is paid off, the momentum of destroying debt is increased, so you will be in this enviable situation in no time.

Your saved dollars can go towards a number of different low-risk investing options. Some options include:

- Standard savings account
- Certificate of deposit (CD)
- Money market account
- 401(k)
- Individual Retirement Account (IRA)

Standard Savings Account

Before looking at other options, don't entirely overlook a standard savings account. There are accounts available now that offer higher interest, especially if you maintain a minimum balance in the account. A standard savings account is still the easiest way to save money and is handy for when you're saving with a purpose in mind, such as for a large purchase. And, unlike some other investing options, your money is always available to be withdrawn, which is a major plus. Setting up a new savings account is literally as easy as walking into the bank and asking for one, and saving accounts are still one of the safest places to keep your money.

Certificate of Deposit (CD)

In this savings arrangement, you loan the bank money (instead of the other way around) and, in turn, are issued a certificate. You are paid a set rate of interest for the bank having access to your funds. These certificates are a relatively safe way to earn money, but they restrict any access to your invested funds until the date of the certificate's maturity. (There's a substantial penalty charged if you need to take your money out early.) These range in length from three months, six months or one to five years. Compare current rates at different financial institutions to see where your certificate of deposit will earn you the most.

Money Market Account

A money market is a short-term mutual fund that invests in products like Treasury bills (which are issued by the government), commercial paper or repurchase agreements. They differ from CDs in that they generally have shorter terms—thirty days to less than one year. These are considered a safe place to plunk your money, and investors often use them to store their money while they're between investing decisions. The benefit is that there is little risk to your investment, but the downside is the yield is considered low. But, you'll still be earning 2–3 percentage points more on average in interest than a high-yielding savings account. With money market funds, you'll often receive a checkbook and can retrieve your funds easily and with no penalty incurred.

401(k)

A 401(k) plan is a retirement savings option that defers money from each of your paychecks. These plans are typically offered as part of a benefits package by employers. With a 401(k) plan, you're deducting from your pre-tax income, so your dollar is worth more when you invest it. If you took that dollar in your paycheck, you'd only receive around eighty cents of it because of taxes. When you put the money into the 401(k) plan, you receive the full dollar. The money is invested in stocks or bonds or cash. It's your choice. Stocks yield the highest return but also present the highest risk. Bonds are more stable but with smaller risk comes smaller returns. Cash is very safe, but you get little to no return at all. The pros of a 401(k) are that you can contribute more money per year than to an IRA, and many employers will match your 401(k) savings up to a certain percent. But there are cons: Your investing options are often set or limited, and you can't always withdraw partial amounts of your money (just the full amount). A 401(k) plan is meant to be a long-term investment that you will access only after you retire. There are penalties for withdrawing from the account early and all of the money in the account is subject to income tax when it is withdrawn.

Individual Retirement Account (IRA)

If your employer doesn't offer a 401(k) plan, you can meet with a financial planner to set up an Individual Retirement Account (IRA). There are two types of IRAs: the Roth and the traditional. The funds you put in an IRA are used toward a number of different types of investment products, like CDs and stocks and bonds, and can usually be withdrawn without penalty. In the Roth IRA plan, your contributions are not tax deductible; all contributions are post-tax. The benefit to contributing post-tax is that because you've already been taxed on the income once, you can't be taxed on it again, and you can withdraw the money tax-free. You usually can access this money at any time, whereas traditional IRA funds can only be accessed after you reach a certain age. (If you withdraw the funds early, you face penalties and fees.) In a traditional IRA, your contributions are tax deductible. You deposit the money from your paycheck into your traditional IRA, and at the end of the year, you can claim your contributions as deductions on your income tax and receive a refund of the taxes you paid on your invested funds. Because you didn't pay taxes when you put the money into the account, you'll have to pay taxes on the money when you withdraw it. Traditional IRAs also have a mandatory withdrawal period, whereas Roth IRAs have no mandatory distribution age. The cons are that there are limitations on who can apply for a Roth IRA: individuals must make $95,000 or less and married couples $150,000 or less to open an account.

Keep in mind as a shopping rule of thumb: Shop with a purpose.

101 FAVORITE MONEY-SAVING TIPS

Here are some of my favorite tips to save you money! Once you get into the swing of spending less, I know you'll come up with at least as many of your own ideas. Keep in mind as a general shopping rule of thumb: Shop with a purpose. Have a list handy and stick to it whenever you're out spending your hard-earned money. Only go shopping when you know what you need, and set a budget for each item you plan to purchase. Try to get out of the habit of shopping just for fun, because, as we've all learned, it's not a lot of fun to pay the consequences for our retail therapy later on.

General Tips

1. **Coupon codes.** Before buying *anything* online do a quick search for coupon codes simply by typing in: "(name of store) + coupon code."

2. **Simply stop shopping.** If you never go to the stores, you won't see irresistible stuff and you won't spend money foolishly. If your favorite shopping is the online variety, find other stuff to do online instead, like browsing through recipes or posting stuff to *sell* on eBay. That's a handy way to turn that shopping urge upside down and make a little money instead.

3. **Return it!** An impulsive buy doesn't necessarily mean long-term consequences. Unless you purchased it on clearance, you can usually return the item with your receipt.

4. **Shop at home for free.** Shopping at home online or via the shopping channel can be a land mine waiting to explode your budget! Instead, try literally shopping at home—go out to the garage, the attic or the storage areas and see what stuff you have lying around that you've totally forgotten about.

5. **Mood lifters.** If you're bummed and need a good laugh or some fun, don't—I repeat *don't*—head to the stores! You'll buy stuff you don't need just to make yourself feel better. Find alternative ways to deal with those emotions, such as talking to a friend or writing out your feelings.

6. **Put it back on the shelf and walk away.** This is the best way to save money while shopping (besides not being in the store in the first place). Put impulse items back on the shelf, then leave the store. If you really feel like you need the item, ask if the store will hold it for a few hours so you have time to simmer down and approach the sale logically, not emotionally. Ask yourself why it suddenly feels so important to own that bracelet or pair of boots.

7. **Have a no-spend day.** When spending is out of control, choosing to have a no-spend day is a fantastic way to get focused

on saving again. Take this challenge to another level by aiming to have five or ten of these in any given month.

8. **TV woes.** TV might be a cheap source of entertainment, but the pull of advertising can wreak havoc on a young family trying to live within a budget. Teach your kids that advertisers are paid to make products look enticing and that the way an item is displayed isn't necessarily how it really looks or works in real life situations.

9. **Dollar store delights.** They might not be the coolest shopping spots around, but we frugalites know that some surprising goodies can be found on these shelves. Just don't overdo it and buy loads of junk just because it's cheap.

10. **Thou art appreciative.** Take a look around you and appreciate what you have, including your friends, family and (hopefully) your health. When you take a good hard look at much of the rest of the world, you'll realize that your life is pretty sweet even if you don't have the biggest house in town.

11. **Reuse almost everything.** Turn it into a challenge for your family to reuse items instead of needlessly throwing them in the trash. You can do so many creative things.

12. **Part-time practicalities.** Getting a part-time job adds to your income and may provide you with a helpful discount. For instance, if you take a job at the supermarket, you'll know when the best sales are on and can snag end-of-day bargains from different departments. Or, if you love clothes, get a job at your favorite store and the discount may be worth just as much as the paycheck you get. For the ultimate benefit, choose a part-time job near your home that you can walk to. Then your transportation costs will be zero.

13. **Make your miles count.** Reward miles and points programs are great, but only if you don't get dinged with ultra-high interest rates. If you collect points or miles, take a good look through the rewards to see which has the most benefit to your family. Sometimes beyond just travel rewards, you can get helpful gift cards for groceries or meals out.

14. **Credit card accountability.** If using credit has gotten out of control, but you just can't stop, take serious measures. Either freeze the card in a plastic container of water *or* keep it with someone you trust (like a parent or spouse) who will demand an explanation when you want to use it again. Either way is harsh, but it works.

15. **Save on interest just by asking**. Call your credit card providers and tell them about a new offer you've received from another bank or company to get lower interest on your credit cards. Ask them to match or beat it. They may at least lower your interest rates in an attempt to retain your account.

16. **Reduce banking fees.** Ask at your bank how you can lower or have no fees attached to your accounts. If you're not satisfied with their answers, you can always switch banks.

17. **Barter.** Instead of paying cash, see if you can barter for items. Check online for bartering in your area to see which local merchants are willing to barter.

18. **Swap.** Swap, don't shop! Find out what stuff you have to swap by doing a major reconnaissance mission in your own closets and storage areas and then have a swap night with friends. This can be a furniture swap, a clothing and accessories swap or even a pantry swap!

19. **Save up change.** A piggy bank can become a substantial

source of savings. Keep saving all your change and then treat yourself to something from the saved coins.

20. **Red pen it.** A red pen is a handy tool in our money-saving arsenal. When you manage to reduce a household expense (like dropping the deluxe satellite TV package for the basic package), use a red pen to strike through the old expense on your budget before you write in the new cost. Once you see those brilliant red lines in a few spots on your budget, you'll get hooked and want to see more costs slashed. It's a great visual reminder, and you'll quickly be able to see where you're saving and where you could save more.

21. **Track your progress.** Make a chart to track your debt reduction or savings growth. Seeing it clearly on a chart will help you keep your goal in mind and encourage you as you see the progress you are making.

22. **Save like it's 1950.** People used to know to save up for any big-ticket item or trip before they purchased it. Take an old-fashioned view and save up your money before going and spending a lot of it. In other words, aim to pay cash instead of credit for all your purchases.

23. **Be gadget conscious.** You might want the latest version of your favorite handheld gadget, but do you need it? The only ones who really benefit are the makers, who rake in cash each time they create a "must-have" update.

24. **Talk it and walk it.** Talking about your new frugal habits can create enthusiasm among your friends and family. Of course, don't talk about it so much that they get sick of hearing it.

25. **Make your frugal ways public.** Some frugalites post a financial blog online to make them accountable. Knowing that a few

hundred people are tracking your debt reduction or savings plan, for example, really keeps one focused on the ultimate goal. Just be sure you don't get too personal and reveal all your financial dirty laundry. Avoid sharing actual figures and actual creditors. Talk in general terms and give updates using percentages—as in "I reached 40 percent of the goal today."

26. **Get to know other frugalities.** If they know how to live within their budget and have fun while doing it, they're useful for you to learn from.

27. **Don't be embarrassed.** Sometimes you'll simply have to say: "I can't afford that." There's no shame in that, especially if your friends know you're working hard to defeat your debt, live within your means or build your savings.

Save on Food

28. **Restaurant halvsies.** Half any meal at a restaurant. You'll be eating a more reasonable portion *and* you can refrigerate the leftovers and have them for lunch the next day. Or, ask the server to serve half of each meal on two different plates and share with a friend. Some restaurants may charge you a dollar or two to split the meal, but it's still much cheaper than paying for two separate entrées.

29. **Restaurant.com.** This is a great resource to save money on any meal out. You can purchase gift certificates at a variety of restaurants for 60 percent off their original value: a twenty-five gift card for only ten bucks. They are redeemable at a wide range of restaurants—go to the Web site to search your area for participating restaurants.

30. **Search for that restaurant online.** Finding the Web sites of your

favorite restaurants can save you money. Check what specials they're currently running or if they have any printable coupons. If so, you might net yourself a free appetizer or dessert, which definitely makes it worth the few minutes it takes to search the Internet.

31. **Lovely lunches don't cost bunches.** If you must dine in a restaurant, then have a meal out during lunchtime instead of supper. Lunches are a bit smaller, but also about 40 percent cheaper—a good tip to keep in mind when travelling.

32. **Raid the pantry, not the supermarket.** Break out of a rut and create new flavor combinations with your next meal by using ingredients you already have in the pantry, fridge and freezer. It will also feel good to know you're not wasting any food.

33. **Build your pantry.** Every week, add a non-perishable item or two to your grocery list. Stock up when they're on sale. Then, when you need to make a meal or two before the next shopping trip, you'll still have ingredients to work with, and you'll have all the essentials you need to make fantastic recipes at home.

34. **Make a meal plan.** Plan your meals for the entire week at one time. Base your menu on items you already have in your pantry and on items you have coupons for, or items that are on sale. Make a complete grocery list using this plan so you'll know exactly what you need to buy at the store. You'll never be at a loss when someone asks "what's for dinner?" and your meal plan will inspire you to dine in instead of dine out.

35. **Grocery lists.** Keep an ongoing list on the fridge all the time and note essentials that you need to restock as you run low on them. Always take a list to the grocery store with you or else you'll return home with impulse buys.

36. **Grocery challenge.** Set a budget for the week and stick to it. Make it a real challenge by trying to spend dramatically less than usual—even half! You'll find the least expensive food is the food you cook from scratch—not the pre-made box or frozen meals.

37. **You can coupon.** Sometimes coupons make a lot of sense. Find a happy medium for your coupon use and clip and save only those you'll really use—then use them when there's a sale for ultimate savings. FPCs (free product coupons) are the ultimate find, so keep an eye peeled for them. Sometimes writing to the company is the best way to net them.

38. **Bring a bag.** Many supermarkets offer cents back if you bring your own bags from home to tote your groceries away. And it's healthier for the earth, too. Keep a selection in your car, in a place where you'll see them, so that you'll actually remember to bring them into the store and use them!

39. **Unit pricing.** If you make a dozen muffins at home, each muffin might cost you a quarter to make. Buying one at the coffee shop could be ten times as much! Knowing the true cost will make that coffee-time snack far less appetizing.

40. **Buy bulk sometimes.** Check the unit pricing to see if buying in bulk really makes sense. Keep track in a grocery price book. Bulk often makes sense for non-perishable items you use often, such as flour or sugar, or items you go through quickly like lunch essentials, snacks or breakfast items.

41. **Grow it yourself.** From beautiful houseplants that add a breath of fresh air to your home, to carrots and spinach and hot peppers out in the garden. Learn how to grow it yourself.

42. **Tote a cooler.** Take a small cooler with you on day trips and

stock it with sandwiches, fresh fruit or chopped veggies, and bottled water, juice or soda. You'll always have a snack and a cold drink without paying premium prices at venues *and* you won't have to wait in line.

43. **DIY ice cream parlor.** Great for kids (or those who never grew up in the first place). Get a tub of vanilla ice cream and then provide an assortment of toppings and sauces taken from your pantry. Baking staples like chocolate chips, coconut and chopped nuts are perfect. A layering of homemade brownies or cookies on the bottom of the bowl turns a regular sundae into something sublime.

44. **Smoothest smoothies.** Smoothies are a luscious treat that hit your wallet hard if you buy them at a juice bar. Instead, keep ingredients on hand to make them at home—frozen fruit, juices, bananas, yogurt. Add a scoop of sorbet if you want a more indulgent treat.

45. **Freezing meals.** Any large-batch cooking becomes budget-friendly when you freeze individual portions to use later. This most obviously applies to casseroles and main meals, but keep it in mind for breakfast meals, too. Your favorite slow-cooking hot cereals can be made in large quantities and then stored in small servings in the freezer, ready to whip out and reheat on a hectic weekday morning. Tuck dinnertime leftovers in individual servings in freezer- and microwave-safe containers to create an easy lunch anytime.

46. **Rethink dinner.** You don't need meat and potatoes at every dinner. A hearty sandwich and a cup of soup makes a great meal, as does an omelette with a slice of toast or pasta.

47. **Eggs-ellent meal potential.** When you're stuck for a low-cost

meal that is yummy and nutritious, it only takes a few eggs to remedy the situation. Anything from a gooey cheese omelette to quiche relies on these staples. Eggs make a great meal at breakfast, at midday or for supper.

48. **Take-out meals at home.** Make it yourself instead of eating out. Whether it's Greek, Vietnamese or Indian, you can find authentic recipes online that allow you to stretch your culinary muscles and delight your taste buds. Once you have some of the basic ingredients, you'll be able to whip up these meals over and over again.

49. **Beyond the brown bag.** Brown bagged lunches sound so sad, like you're depriving yourself of a nice midday meal. Spark up your lunches by taking wholesome salads with a boost of protein—like chicken, tuna or chickpeas—or last night's leftovers to heat up the next day. Just because you brown-bag it doesn't mean you have to stick with boring sandwiches.

50. **Rotisserie me.** Deli chickens at the supermarket make for a fast, nutritious and easy meal minus the price of a sit-down dinner. They're not the cheapest option, but if it's mealtime *now* and you want to prevent another trip to the family's favorite restaurant, these will do the trick nicely. You'll save on sides and drinks. For the price of one individual meal out, you'll be able to feed your entire family. Use leftovers the next day for chicken salad sandwiches or as added protein to your favorite salad.

51. **Rice it up.** Rice is a staple you should always have in the pantry. It's a simple side dish, makes for creamy rice pudding and can even be ground up into gluten-free flour!

52. **Greens.** Nutrient dense greens—from spinach to beet greens

and beyond—are usually a bargain in the produce department. They are great in soups or cooked simply with a little olive oil, garlic and salt and pepper. Or, purée them and add them to other sauces for hidden additional nutrition that your kids won't suspect.

53. **A pasta affair.** Keep a selection of pasta in the pantry all the time for quick meals. It's ideal served simply, like with a tomato sauce or mixed with steamed veggies, olive oil and Parmesan cheese.

54. **Charming chickpeas.** A can or bag of these is a meal just waiting to be born. Use these in place of meat in any of your favorite recipes, especially curries, where the creaminess of the chickpeas and the hot spices seem a perfect match. Keep cans on hand all the time. A handful of chickpeas will also add fiber and protein to any salad.

55. **Buy a stainless steel water bottle.** Use this every day instead of buying bottled water and you'll save hundreds of dollars a year. Plus, the metal is safer because no plastic can leach into your drink. And think of all environmental costs you're saving by not consuming disposable bottles.

56. **Say no to processed.** Some people swear that it's cheaper to eat a lot of mixes and pre-made stuff, but I don't believe it. Buy a few whole potatoes instead of a package of mashed potato mix, or a bag of whole carrots to peel and slice yourself instead of prechopped and peeled baby carrots. Plus, whole foods are much healthier than processed. The sodium alone can be a huge problem in processed food.

57. **Bake it**. Baking cookies, breads and other treats at home saves money *and* ensures that the best ingredients are used.

Save on Beauty

58. Spa-licious. Maybe a day at your favorite spa isn't in the budget this month (or year!). But, you can re-create the serenity of a spa at home. Plan ahead, get a sitter for the kids (barter with a friend or relative for those services for extra savings), and linger in a steamy bath with candles lit all around the tub. Give yourself a home manicure and pedicure. Lounge on your couch in your robe and read your favorite magazine.

59. Make mine a four-in-one. Those popular three-in-one bath formulas (they work as shampoo, body wash or bubble bath) also work to fill your soap dispenser! A four-in-one product is a fantastic money saver because you're buying one product to take the place of four others. At the discount stores, you can purchase deliciously scented one-liter bottles of these for a few bucks.

60. Scarf-able. Scarves can be swooped around your neck or tied around your waist as a makeshift belt. They can completely change the look and style of any outfit. Plus, they can brighten up home décor, too, bringing new life to throw pillows.

61. Revamped shoes. Ho-hum shoes get a facelift by popping on a pair of clip-on earrings! This can change the look of an old pair of shoes into something stylish, especially if the budget won't stretch to buy a new pair.

62. Make panty hose last. Freeze them! Store new panty hose in the freezer and don't be surprised when family members tease you about it. Silliness aside, this really does work to strengthen the fibers and make these budget busters last.

63. Buttons and beads. These can be used in a multitude of creative ways: for jewelry, for enhancing clothing or for making accessories sizzle. Get them at the dollar store or at second-hand shops where you'll find some beautiful old buttons, often in a big bag. Or, hit up the thrift store and buy some very inexpensive clothing items that have great buttons that can be removed.

64. **Chic in black.** Or whatever color you love (or flatters you) the most. By having a theme color for your wardrobe, you can mix and match with ease and don't need to buy as many clothes overall.

Save Around the House

65. **Mortgage minded.** As in paying it off way faster! Paying every two weeks can shave a couple of years off your overall mortgage and save you thousands.

66. **Help your landlord.** Sometimes your time and energy can equal a lower rent payment each month. It never hurts to ask if your landlord needs help shovelling snow or mowing grass.

67. **Dishwasher dos.** Save by running your dishwasher at night, when electricity costs less. Turn it on just before you head to bed. Try using plain white vinegar as a replacement for commercial rinse agent.

68. **Warranty wisdom.** The warranty that comes with any new purchase is there for a reason, so use it! Register your products with the manufacturer and keep a file folder of warranties with the original sales receipt stapled to it. If an appliance breaks down, contact the manufacturer. Be careful before throwing money away on pricey *extended* warranties, which retailers offer and can make a lot of money from. If the product is generally reliable, it makes sense to say no to the

extended warranty. (To find out if the product is reliable, be sure to do your research first and discover what consumers are saying about it. You'll still receive a general warranty, which often lasts one year.)

69. **Sunshiny day.** A blast of sunshine flowing through the windows not only eases your electric bill, but it makes you feel good. Open up those curtains and let the sunshine in all over the place.

70. **Power strips are power-less.** This is a great tip for the home office—hook up a power strip to all the stuff that uses electrical juice: the computer, fax, printer, etc. Then, when you want to de-juice it all at once, you only need to turn off one switch. Do the same with your entertainment center. You'd be surprised by how much electricity your office equipment and home electronics continue to use even when they are turned off.

71. **Install shower heads that save on water.** For a small investment, you can save more than half the water flowing through your old shower heads.

72. **Don't flush so much!** I can almost hear you saying "Ewwww" from here, but it's not what you think. Make your toilet more water-efficient. Toilet flushes account for 40 percent of your home's water usage. If your toilet was made before 1992, it could use up to seven gallons of water per flush! Consider replacing the toilet with a more water-efficient model. If that's not in the budget, there are kits available that can help you improve your toilet's efficiency. The best part is you don't have to be a plumber to install them.

73. **Lights off.** If your family members have a hard time

remembering to turn off a light switch when they leave the room, check out automatic timers that do it for them. Ask at any hardware or build-it center for details on these devices.

74. **Earth and budget friendly light bulbs.** New energy efficient light bulbs outshine their predecessors by providing light without added heat, thereby using only a third of the energy. Some studies show that lighting your home accounts for 20 percent of your electric bill, so this a worthwhile change to make.

> **Toilet flushes account for 40 percent of your home's water usage. If your toilet was made before 1992, it could use up to seven gallons of water per flush!**

75. **Buy pay-as-you-go cell minutes.** This will keep your cell phone usage reasonable. When the minutes are out, so is your cell phone until you have the money to add more minutes.

76. **Paint possibilities.** A can of paint can revitalize a lot of surfaces. Keep an eye out for freebie paint to be had, such as when a neighbor or friend has repainted and is stuck with extra cans.

77. **Add color.** When you're in the mood to redecorate, but your bank account begs to differ, add a flash of flavor to any room simply by adding splashes of color. You can reinvent a whole space this way by choosing an accent color with some serious attitude, like a bright lime green or tangerine orange.

78. **Wallpaper patches.** Wallpaper can be a major statement in a room, but it can be costly and it's a lot of work. Get the impact without the cost or effort by putting wallpaper samples in large frames. You could even use funky fabric or wrapping

paper instead. Paint wrapping paper with a clear matte finish sealant to take the shine off.

79. **Sew what?** Sewing is a handy hobby. You can make creative outfits and home décor elements with ease. Blankets, pillowcases and curtains don't require patterns (which can be pricey) and make great gifts.

80. **Soap and water.** Pricey cleaners don't necessarily clean any better than good old soap and water. A squirt of dishwashing liquid in a bucket of water will clean nearly anything.

81. **Multipurpose products.** The more uses any product has, the less you'll spend on other stuff. One example is to buy gentle dishwashing liquid that doubles as hand soap. It can also be used as a general, all-purpose cleaner when combined with water in a squirt bottle and as a pretreater for laundry stains. Baking soda is the ultimate example—about a hundred different uses in one little box.

82. **Two sensible cleaners.** One part white vinegar to three or four parts water is an ultra cheap cleaner to replace multipurpose cleaners around your home. And yes, that vinegar aroma will dissipate quickly, I promise. For more disinfecting power, try 3 percent hydrogen peroxide on kitchen and bath surfaces.

83. **Gas grade.** You don't always need the best grade of gas, so check the owner's manual that came with the vehicle for the recommended grade.

84. **Tinker under the hood.** Learning some basic car maintenance will save you loads. Change your own oil, replace burnt out signal lights and headlights or barter with a friend who is mechanically inclined.

85. **Buy one-year-old (or older) vehicles.** Most depreciation in

vehicles happens in the first year. Brand-new vehicles lose value as soon as you drive them off the lot. Spend less and protect your investment by purchasing vehicles that are at least one year old.

86. **Long live the gas tank.** Challenge yourself to make a tank of gas last longer. Plan outings so that all your errands are done in one logical circle, not backtracking needlessly. Carpool whenever possible.

Save on Entertainment

87. **Beach adventure.** Find great swimming spots near where you live. Check on a season rate for the public pool in your city. If you live near beaches, take advantage of them. If you're landlocked and in a rural setting, use a friend's pool or pond, with their permission. Ask them which days and times are acceptable for you to swim (like Monday afternoons or Thursday mornings). Just be sure not to abuse the privilege.

88. **Free activities.** Make a master list of free stuff to do around your town. When you see an event advertised in the paper, cut it out or write it down. Involve your family in this one to create a huge list of fun stuff to do minus the cost.

89. **Free movies.** A quick jaunt to your local library is all it takes to get a DVD for free, and you'll usually have longer to view it than if you'd rented it from the video store. Or swap movies with friends.

90. **Video game savings.** Video game lovers can save by buying secondhand games online or at local consignment game stores. Take your own games in for credit towards new games. When you want a new gaming system altogether, sell

your old system along with the games to take a dent out of
the cost of the new one.

91. **Board—not bored—games.** Find them at a yard sale for a buck
or two and then make it a family night tradition. Or, have a
card tournament at your place and when your friends ask if
they can bring some snacks, say yes.

92. **Socialize, don't spend.** Instead of going out to eat, have a
potluck at your place with your best buddies. Or, whip up a
batch of cupcakes and have some of your children's friends
over to decorate them.

93. **Book it.** Book lovers' needs are few—just a great book in
hand, and no matter what the weather is, we're happy as
literary clams. Get your book fix by swapping with friends
or heading to the library. Secondhand stores sometimes have
sales where you can fill a bag with books for about ten dollars
—a great bargain indeed! And boxes of books are always
available for cents at garage sales.

94. **Lovin' the library.** Your local library is a hot spot for cheap
entertainment (besides books and movies), especially for the
kids. Check out their free programs for children by asking
for a schedule of events and activities.

Save on Vacations and Celebrations

95. **Book it online.** Save on vacations just by booking online
instead of using a 1-800 number because the Web site is
automated.

96. **Vacation like you live there.** Renting a condo at your vacation
destination can be far cheaper than a posh hotel room. Plus,
you'll have the added benefit of a full kitchen, which will

make it easy to at least make breakfast at home (and possibly a picnic lunch) every day, thus saving you more money.

97. **Ask around for cheap eats.** Whether on vacation or at home, ask freely for advice on where to get great food for cheap. Locals always know the hottest eating spots. All you have to do is ask.

98. **Great atmosphere creates great gatherings.** Any room or area in your home can be made party-worthy with a little work. Rearrange furniture and ask friends to bring funny photos to add to the light-hearted mood.

99. **Say it with a picture.** A framed photo is always a thoughtful gift. Reuse an old photo frame or fix up a plain one from the dollar store. Use a bit of spray paint or embellishments to personalize the frame to match the photo or the personality of the recipient. Sometimes older frames are more fabulous because they have more character.

100. **Give a gift of time (or assistance).** When the budget doesn't stretch to allow for lovely store-bought gifts, give a gift of your time or help.

101. **Gather gift cards.** When money is tight, these can be useful to buy the stuff you really need, even groceries or a meal out. They also make easy gifts by regifting them if you're stuck needing a gift and don't have a cent to spend on one.

Living large on less means changing how you feel about your life and living it within a budget. It means keeping track of your spending—one of the hardest habits to develop at first, but one of the most beneficial in reducing debt and curbing overspending. The largest lived lives are ones lived richly, but within one's means. So, go live it!

Appendix

GOAL SETTING CHART

Goal setting comes in all shapes, sizes and varieties. You could be saving for a major purchase, a vacation, education or retirement. You might also be saving for an emergency fund or paying down debt. The total cost is the total amount of money you intend to spend. The target date is when you would like to achieve this goal. The monthly contribution is the amount of money you will devote to this goal each month. Divide your total cost by the number of months left until your target date to find how much your monthly contribution needs to be. If your budget won't accommodate this monthly figure, move the target date out until you reach a figure that you can realistically contribute.

GOAL SETTING CHART

GOAL	Total Cost	Target Date	Monthly Contribution	Bonus Contribution
	$		$	$
	$		$	$
	$		$	$
	$		$	$
	$		$	$
	$		$	$
	$		$	$
	$		$	$
	$		$	$
	$		$	$

DEBT REDUCTION CHART

Having the information about your personal debt at hand makes it easier to track and eventually conquer. List all types of debt, the amount owing and current interest rates. You'll assign each debt an order of repayment number: 1 being first, 2 being second, etc.

When deciding the order of repayment of your debt, keep two factors in mind:

1. Is it a short- or long-term debt? (Meaning, can you pay the debt off in a matter of a few months? Or, will it take longer?)
2. What is the interest rate you're currently paying on this debt?

Generally, the highest interest debts are the ones you'll want to pay down first because you'll save overall on high interest charges. But, if you have some small debts that you can pay off quickly, tackle them first to give you a good head start on your debt reduction goals. It'll give you a boost to know you've already defeated some of your debt!

For more tips on defeating debt faster, refer back to chapter three.

DEBT REDUCTION CHART

Debt	Amount Owing	Interest Rate	Minimum Contribution	Order of Payment
	$	%	$	
	$	%	$	
	$	%	$	
	$	%	$	
	$	%	$	
	$	%	$	
	$	%	$	
	$	%	$	
	$	%	$	
	$	%	$	
	$	%	$	

Index

Books of Interest

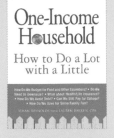

365 Ways to Live Cheap

Take a look at your life and you'll realize that there's almost always a way to make do on less. This book offers up a bevy of ways to cut down on costs and still enjoy a satisfying lifestyle in any situation. From practicing good gas conservation habits to learning to love leftovers, this book will help every aspiring penny pincher stop the unnecessary spending and find the fun in frugality.
ISBN-13: 978-1-60550-042-3; ISBN-10: 1-60550-042-9; paperback, 240 pages, #Z2898

One-Income Household: How to Do a Lot with a Little

This book offers practical, easy-to-apply advice your family can tailor to your personal situation, whether your income status is by choice or by forced circumstances. You'll find help with budgeting for essentials, securing health insurance, paying down debt, finding affordable housing and more.
ISBN-13: 978-1-60550-133-8; ISBN-10: 1-60550-133-6; paperback, 256 pages, #Z3077

Suddenly Frugal

Looking for realistic ways to save money on everyday expenses? Look no further. Financial whiz Leah Ingram will help you identify small, painless changes you can make to your daily spending habits. You'll also find ways to inspire your family members to go frugal and learn how to work as a team when it comes to family finances.
ISBN-13: 978-1-4405-0182-1; ISBN-10: 1-4405-0182-3; paperback, 256 pages, #Z5727

**These books and other fine F+W Media titles are available at your local bookstore or from online suppliers.
Visit our website at _____ ooks.com.**